REFLECTIONS
ON THE
BRAZILIAN
COUNTER-REVOLUTION

REFLECTIONS ON THE BRAZILIAN COUNTER-REVOLUTION

ESSAYS BY FLORESTAN FERNANDES

Edited with an introduction by Warren Dean

M. E. Sharpe, Inc.

Armonk, New York

HN
287
.F413
1981

The essays by Florestan Fernandes in this volume are translated and
published here by arrangement with the author.

Translated from the Portuguese by Michel Vale and Patrick M. Hughes.

Library of Congress Cataloging in Publication Data

Fernandes, Florestan.
　　Reflections on the Brazilian counter-revolution.

　　Translated from Portuguese.
　　"Published simultaneously as volume XI, 1-2 of International
journal of sociology."
　　"Bibliography: selected writings of Florestan Fernandes": p.
　　Contents: On the formation and development of the competitive social
order—The autocratic-bourgeois model of capitalist transformation—
Revolution or counter-revolution?—[etc.]
　　　　1. Brazil—Social conditions—Addresses, essays, lectures. 2. Social
structure—Brazil—Addresses, essays, lectures. 3. Social change—
Addresses, essays, lectures. 4. Fernandes, Florestan—Bibliography.
I. Dean, Warren. II. Title.
HN287.F413　1981　　　981　　　80-5456
ISBN 0-87332-177-4　　　　　　AACR2

Printed in the United States of America

CONTENTS

INTRODUCTION

Florestan Fernandes is Brazil's most distinguished sociologist. He comes from the generation of social scientists trained in the early years of the Faculty of Philosophy, Sciences, and Letters of the University of São Paulo. It was then the refuge of several of France's greatest intellects, including Claude Levi-Strauss, Roger Bastide, Fernand Braudel, and Charles Morazé. Fernandes went on to gain the doctorate with a thesis in ethnohistory ("The Social Organization of the Tupinambá," 1947). This and a second monograph dealing with that tribe ("The Social Function of War in Tupinambá Society") are regarded as among the finest in Brazilian ethnographic literature. Fernandes went on to teach in the Chair of Sociology I at the same Faculty, and collaborated with Bastide in a study of race relations ("Race Relations between Blacks and Whites in São Paulo") which remains essential reading in that field. By 1964 Fernandes had won the competition for Professor Catedrático with another thesis on race ("The Integration of the Negro in Class Society"), a work later translated into English in an abridged version. Meanwhile Fernandes produced monographs on the training and concerns of Brazilian social scientists, the empirical foundations of sociological inquiry, the sociology of education, and urban folklore.

The first twenty years of his professional career were immensely productive of students as well. An entire generation of sociologists was formed in his classes, some of them scholars of global reputation, well known through translations, including Fernando Henrique Cardoso, Octavio Ianni, Luiz Pereira, Juarez Brandão Lopes, Marialice Foracchi, Leoncio Martins Rodrigues, Gabriel Bolaffi, Maria Sylvia Carvalho Franco, Roberto Cardoso de Oliveira, José de Souza Martins, Gabriel Cohn, and many others of equal accomplishments and merit. His influence and inspiration are evident in their writings and, to his great intellectual credit, so is their continuing influence reflected in his work. The result has been, over the years, an engrossing dialogue wherein Fernandes's voice appears as fresh and vigorous as those of his students, or even of his students' students.

Some of the social scientists of São Paulo were caught up in the 1950s and early 1960s in the tremendous political debates and organizing activity that marked Brazil's rapid economic and social transformation. These sincere and intelligent efforts were dashed by the coup staged by the military in March 1964. With this intervention the university, like the labor unions, the press, the courts, and the political system itself, was subjected to repeated interference. Student unions were declared illegal, publications were banned, deans and rectors were removed, to be replaced by hirelings, and police informers were put in the classrooms. The campus was invaded, students were jailed and expelled. Fernandes continued, nevertheless, to challenge the military, not only in his writings but also in the great moral authority of his presence in the university and in his outspoken and contentious opinions, which he unhesitatingly expressed. Finally in 1969, as part of a sweeping series of authoritarian measures, hundreds of professors were forcibly retired, among them Florestan Fernandes.

He had already been welcomed, by Charles Wagley in 1965-66, as a visiting professor at Columbia University. In 1969 he became a resident scholar, and then professor, at the University of Toronto. Nonetheless, he returned to Brazil to teach, as he could, principally at PUC—the Catholic Pontifical University of São Paulo—which as a private school was still allowed to hire an internal exile. He received further invitations to teach in the United States, at Yale and Columbia. Finally, in 1978, the worst of the repression was over. As other Brazilians began returning home, Fernandes became a full-time professor at PUC.

After the military coup, Fernandes had turned to the study of contemporary social structure and social change. It is hardly necessary to point out the urgency of such a task in a country where a class dictatorship had been imposed, or the special meaning of this study to reformers, who had aspired after a transformation that would engender a more just society and who had suffered ignominy because that aspiration had become, officially, a punishable offense—a breach of national security, no less. To some degree, committed social scientists even felt a sense of failure, for the intervention had not been generally expected and the imposition of an authoritarian, army-ruled regime was entirely unforeseen. Fernandes's later writings therefore contain a radical engagement with a hideous reality, an attempt to come to terms with it and to find a way out of that terrible impasse.

This collection of essays in translation is devoted to writings from this more recent area of concern. Although they are not well known abroad, these works are important for an understanding of the present and the proximate future of Brazil. In them Fernandes makes significant theoretical contributions, especially in his synthesis of structural-functionalism and Marxian social analysis and in his reconceptualizations in dependency theory. A more complex rendering is to be found here of the evolution of Brazilian society, and the "bourgeois revolution" is specified more closely and analytically than in any other recent synthetic account.

Fernandes's approach is developmental and therefore historical. His references will pose a challenge for the non-Brazilian reader, for that country's remarkable historical trajectory is little known abroad. Although some explanatory notes have been provided, they are no doubt too slight to clarify events sufficiently. A few more guideposts are offered here.

*   *   *

Brazil was a Portuguese colony from 1500 to 1822. Land grants were made on a vast scale in order to install immediately a creole aristocracy. The colony was organized to produce sugar and exploit gold deposits, mainly with African slave labor since the native Americans were decimated by disease and marauding settlers. Portuguese control was assured partly through submission of the metropolis to English economic domination. When João VI fled Lisbon in 1807, a jump ahead of Napoleon's invading army, and came to Rio de Janeiro, in effect he transferred the seat of sovereignty. When he returned in 1820, the Brazilian landed classes were impelled to proclaim his son Pedro emperor of an independent Brazil.

The empire maintained slavery and extended the reach of the plantation system. It was sustained by exports of coffee from the region of Rio de Janeiro. This program was decidedly modest and transitional, and the empire, even though stable compared to Spanish America, was quite weak. It may not have experienced any economic growth until shortly before its demise, in 1889. The supply of Africans was cut off by British pressure, in 1850. Thereafter the slave population tended to decline. The discovery that European immigrants would come to work the coffee plantations if their passage was paid by the government was nearly fortuitous and coincided with slavery's final collapse in 1888.

The export-producing planters and their banker and importer allies remained influential in the Republic, but as Fernandes shows, an evolution was occurring, driven by world market forces and the emerging monopolistic structures, and by internal developments as well. Tariffs, the main source of government funds because of upper-class objections to land or income taxes, had to be raised because of rising government obligations, largely to English banks. The outcome was a small industrial sector, mainly in consumer goods. Abolition and immigration both stimulated city growth, and exports paid for the installation of rails, ports, and telegraph. The republican presidents succeeded each other in outwardly liberal-democratic style. But the elections were rigged, as they had been under the empire, and only 5 to 10 percent of adults voted. The labor movement was illegal and severely repressed.

With the collapse of sugar and the world trading system, the "Old" Republic fell in 1930. It was replaced by a "revolutionary" government led by Getulio Vargas, once governor of Rio Grande do Sul state. A long period of crisis followed, in which increasingly centralist, corporativist, and autarkic policies were implemented within an authoritarian framework. Vargas in 1937 imposed a fascistic "Estado Novo," but was nevertheless welcomed as a wartime ally by the United States. He was overthrown by his generals in 1945, largely because he was thought to be leaning too much on his controlled labor organization. A liberal-democratic constitution was written, parties formed, and one general-candidate defeated another at the polls. The new regime favored middle-class consumption aspirations and a restoration of export orientation. The Communist Party was again outlawed. Then Vargas returned, was elected president, and followed a nationalist and pro-labor course. The state petroleum company, Petrobrás, was formed and other statist measures were foreshadowed. Vargas became the object of a press campaign focusing on the corruption of his subordinates; he committed suicide in 1954, before the generals could again depose him.

The next elected president was Juscelino Kubitschek, former governor of Minas Gerais state. Kubitschek relied on rapid economic growth via import substitution as his means of retaining office. He invited multinational corporations to install auto and other industries. His successor, former São Paulo governor Janio Quadros, struggled with the inflation provoked by Kubitschek's financing, but was frustrated by the limited power of the presidency. He resigned from office, expecting a popular reaction to call him back. Instead his vice-president, João Goulart, took over and resumed essentially Vargasist policies. Once again a crisis developed, fueled by the example of Cuba and the organizing of larger sectors of labor, including rural workers. The military swept Goulart from power in 1964 and, in contrast to the pattern of their earlier interventions, they remained in control.

This regime reached the height of its authoritarian sway and the maximum of its élan and self-confidence during the so-called economic "miracle," from 1967 to 1974. At the time it was widely regarded, in fact, as a political "model" for other less developed countries to follow to achieve capitalist economic development: baldly put, a judicious combination of terror against dissidents, wage rises below inflation rates for the masses, and windfall favors for entrepreneurs. The "miracle" faded considerably after the first round of OPEC price increases, since Brazil could supply not more than a small fraction of its oil requirements. Fernandes's book *The Bourgeois Revolution in Brazil*, excerpted here, therefore reflects upon the autocratic bourgeois state at its moment of grandeur. By the time of the writing of "Revolution or Counter-Revolution?" the regime was coming noticeably unglued. The tendency has continued unabated, so that Fernandes's ideas have served as an important contribution to the debate over positions that the popular forces might adopt in confronting the current situation.

* * *

The editor has not treated these articles and chapters as texts calling invariably for a word-by-word translation. The material has occasionally been edited for conciseness, in an endeavor to enhance its meaning. The concepts, however, have been consistently rendered. The editor greatly appreciates the painstaking efforts of the translators, Michel Vale and Patrick Hughes. We were aware of the responsibility we shared in transposing into English a significant sample of the thought of one of Brazil's most important social scientists. We hope the result is of use to other scholars who are at the same time participants in the great transformations that both "center" and "periphery" will yet undergo.

The editor also wishes to acknowledge the assistance of several persons who commented on the selection and significance of Fernandes's works, especially Antonio Carlos Bernardo, Gabriel Bolaffi, Fernando Henrique Cardoso, Anna Maria Corrêa, Ulysses Guariba, Jaime Pinsky, and Liliana Sobron. Professor Fernandes himself gave me access to his library and permission to reprint whatever we wished. That I was able to begin the work in Brazil was due to a travel grant from the American Philosophical Society's Penrose Fund.

Warren Dean

REFLECTIONS
ON THE
BRAZILIAN
COUNTER-REVOLUTION

ON THE FORMATION
AND DEVELOPMENT OF
THE COMPETITIVE
SOCIAL ORDER

As capitalism is absorbed as a system of relations of production and exchange, a typical social order evolves which organizes institutionally a framework for the dynamic equilibrium inherent in the integration, functioning, and differentiation of that system, and adapts it to economic and sociocultural potentialities. This social order has been dubbed by historians, economists, sociologists, jurists, and political scientists the *competitive social order*. Here we shall be interested solely in those aspects of its emergence and development that are structurally characteristic of the bourgeois revolution in Brazil.

In dependent "national societies" of colonial origin, capitalism is introduced *before* the competitive social order is constituted. It has to confront economic, social, and political structures elaborated under the colonial regime and only partially and superficially adapted to capitalist patterns of economic life. As the colonial regime breaks down, these structures permit and further adaptation to the dynamics of the world market, which in reality determine this transition and serve as the base on which an "independent" national economy gradually takes shape. The intensity and the structural or dynamic effects of this phase depend on the economic, cultural, and political heritage handed down from the colonial period. In Latin America this period has, as a rule, assumed the pattern of a long-term evolution in those countries that were able to organize and swiftly expand a relatively differentiated and integrated internal market on capitalist foundations. This means that,

From *A Revolução Burguesa no Brasil: Ensaio de Interpretação* (Rio de Janeiro: Zahar Editores, 1976), pp. 149-97.

over a period of some three-quarters of a century to a century or more, the economic, social, and political structures inherited from the colonial world progressively meshed with the dynamics of the world market, selectively screening its positive effects and restraining its constructive impact on internal economic growth. Strictly speaking, these structures were useful only because they served— wherever such a thing could occur on an effective scale—the historical function of keeping vital economic decisions in national hands.

In general, Brazil fits this pattern. The economic, social, and political structures of its colonial society not only molded the later national society; they also determined, over both the short and the long term, the proportions and scope of the economic dynamics absorbed from the world market. These structures proved to be quite malleable under the impact of what might be called the reorganization of the colonial market. They adapted rapidly to the two poles of the business of exporting and importing, controlled economically by an external hegemonic center but steered politically from within. Nonetheless, these same structures proved resistant and at times even rigid when it came to absorbing the economic dynamics that were key to the internal expansion of capitalism. Here, the effectiveness of the external determining factors in achieving their purpose over the short and long term depended on the speedy erosion of the colonial structures of economic, social, and political life. Some idea of the degree of resistance encountered may be derived from the position that England was forced to assume in combatting slavery and the slave trade and from the conflicts ensuing from that struggle. Thus the screening of dynamic influences from the world market followed a relatively rigid line, determined to a large extent by the economic interests of the agrarian aristocracy. These interests were counterbalanced to only a very minor and secondary degree by the economic interests of the specifically commercial sector, linked to the import business. The limiting effects of this situation on the intensity and internal development of capitalism can be readily appreciated (even without invoking comparisons with the economic development of the United States). Nonetheless it is also clear that this process helped to safeguard, principally at the political level,[1] the territorial integrity of the country and the relative autonomy of its internal economic growth.

Two things are suggested by these considerations. First, the slavocratic and seigneurial social order did not easily accommodate to the economic, social, cultural, and juridical-political require-ments of capitalism. Even when these became a part of the legal in-frastructure of that order, they were doomed to ineffectiveness or received but partial and fluctuating attention in accordance with what the seigneurial ranks* found to be economically useful (which in turn was to a large extent determined and gauged by the eco-nomic, social, and political structures inherited from the colonial world). Second, the competitive social order emerged gradually, as the disintegration of the slavocratic and seigneurial social order provided solid stepping stones for a genuinely capitalist reorganiza-tion of the relations of production and of the market. We see, then, that the difficulties encountered by capitalism in its internal expansion did not always derive from "resistance to change" by the seigneurial ranks. It is the "peripheral" and "marginal" situa-tion of dependent capitalist economies of colonial origin which ac-counts for this phenomenon, with all its dynamic and structural repercussions on the competitive social order.

In the present essay we shall be directly interested in both as-pects, in terms of the emergence and consolidation of a competi-tive style of social existence, not the mere disappearance of the seigneurial style. Thus three basic topics will be focused upon: (a) the conditions, tensions, or inconsistencies of the slavocratic and seigneurial social order which turned competition into a dy-namic factor; (b) the nature and effect of the economic and socio-cultural processes responsible for the universalization of the com-petitive social order; (c) the structural and functional character-istics of the competitive social order under dependent capitalism and their significance for the emergence of a style specific to the bourgeois revolution.

As regards the first point, we know that the social order in-herent in the slavocratic and seigneurial society was hardly propi-tious to the development of competition as a basic structural and dynamic factor of social life. Even so, its influence was certainly not absent in points of tension and association of a competitive nature, among persons or groups of persons. Nonetheless, power was organized at the economic, social, and cultural levels in such a

---

Estamento is here translated as "estate" when unqualified, and as "rank" when qualified, e.g., "middling rank(s)"—*estamento(s) intermediario(s); estamental, estamentais* (adj.) is translated as "of the estate," "estate-like," "estate-bound," etc.—Ed.

way as to absorb these points of tension and association, and thus to diminish the importance of competition in the typically seigneurial forms of socialization, human interaction, and social control. Competition had some structural and functional significance only because traditional patrimonial domination obliged the clans, as groups or through their heads, to engage in continuous emulation in the struggle to preserve or augment their wealth, social prestige, and power. It did not appear as a distinct process, socially perceived or valued as such. On the contrary, it constituted a structural and dynamic component of the social obligations and responsibilities that bound men to each other and to the *senhor* in their actions, their persons, and their lives, through traditions, the duty to command or to obey, and through moral solidarity. The factors that went to make up such emulation in the struggle for wealth, social prestige, and power did not disappear with political emancipation. The absorption of patrimonial domination by the estates meant a shift from authority to a specifically political form of power. As a consequence, clans and kinship alliances intensified the traditionally accepted forms of personal or group competition. Since the established order did not undergo any fundamental transformations of social structure, conventions, the traditional code of honor, and the mechanisms of patrimonial domination continued to dilute and neutralize the competitive elements, maintaining an emphasis on cooperation and on autocratic forms of solidarity as factors of social equilibrium.

Had the political revolution set into motion by independence also been a social and economic revolution, events would have taken a different course. The competitive social order would have emerged together with the nation state and with the upsurge of modernization following the direct incorporation of the Brazilian economy into the world market. Nonetheless, the absorption of patrimonial domination by the establishment represented *de facto* the surmounting of those material and moral conditions which until then had blocked the unfolding of the full potentialities of the slavocratic and seigneurial order. As paradoxical as it may seem, the social order constructed under the colonial regime was to demonstrate its historical efficacity under the regime of national independence.

However, this did not keep it from experiencing certain disintegrating influences, within the historical context of an emerging national society and under the growing pressure of governing dynamics of the world economy that had been internally absorbed as institutions. As regards the sociological significance of competition, its main impact was felt as structural-functional discrepancies within the system of status and social roles, as a relative lack of flexibility in the social order itself.

In a society of castes or estates that has maintained its equilibrium and development, the focal points of social tension most important for the continuance of the established order are to be found in the privileged and dominant social strata. These strata have the means to "make" history and to alter the "normal course of events." This was especially true of the rural aristocracy, which itself generated the seeds of disintegration and destruction of the slavocratic and seigneurial social order on account of insoluble tensions in the internal structure of its privileged world affecting the social fate of the *senhor*—and not that of the slave, the freedman, or the dependent free worker. At least three kinds of tension merit discussion in the present study: the contradiction between the material foundations and the legitimation of the seigneurial status; the discrepancies between "attributed status" and "real status" in the middling ranks; and finally the value conflict between the ideal norms and the practical norms guiding the social role of the *senhor*. As long as slavocratic and seigneurial society was able to dilute and neutralize these tensions, they did not affect its equilibrium. Nonetheless, once that ceased to be the case, these tensions served to undermine the structure of that society and to counter its inner dynamics. They dismantled it as though it had been an entirely artificial construct, precipitating the emergence, from within, of social forms that negated its real and ideal foundations, ultimately to destroy it.

The first kind of tension has already been analyzed in various contexts in the preceding discussion [in part one of *A Revolução Burguesa no Brasil*]: from the negation of the bourgeois condition in favor of seigneurial status (during the period of national liberation), to the negation of seigneurial status in favor of the bourgeois condition (during the final disintegration of the slave system and of imperial society). The points we have discussed do not imply that it was impossible to reconcile capitalism with the existence of a patrimonial and autocratic rural aristocracy. They indicate only that this combination could not persist indefinitely under internal and external conditions that spelt doom to the survival of the rural aristocracy as such. What is interesting about the course of events described are the changes that took place in the cast of mind and the behavior of the most privileged economic actors in the slave economy. At stake was not the social, political, and economic privileges accruing to them by virtue of social position, but the social system of slavery which guaranteed this position (and which they hoped to change without any risk to their privileges). Their view of history was to be that the social order, not they, had been at fault. Hence, in the final stage of this course of events, the ruling estates and their elites preferred a political solution which, by means of the Republic, adapted society to its bourgeois condition. Though they went about things differently, the style and the values inspiring them were the same as those that politically guided the seigneurial ranks and their elites during the period of national liberation.

What is known about this sociohistorical and political context shows that the *senhor* did not assimilate either immediately or quickly the "creative rationality" some sociologists impute to the "spirit of capitalism." The lessons of experience taught him two things. First, that the real basis of his power did not derive from the free play of the market, but from his key position in the control of the economy and society. Second, that all his power was insufficient to alter the dynamics, the fluctuations, and the pressures of the world market—"hard realities" that could be confronted only internally. Thus a struggle transcending the national society had to be joined and won within that society's structures. This meant that the economic context, shaped by the internal expansion of capitalism, shifted the focus of personal and group competition for wealth, social prestige, and power. Economic dynamics regulated by the world market reached the very core of the seigneurial condition: they acted from within upon the interests, the avenues of power, and the world view of the *senhor*. He may have been unable to extricate himself entirely from the web of obligations, duties, and responsibilities linked to patrimonial rule and the patriarchal family, and to localism and traditionalism. Nonetheless, little by little the *senhor*, as an economic actor, surmounted these limitations and attempted to meet head on those external influences that were determining his economic fate and the material foundations of his position of power within the national society. The coffee farmers in the Vale do Paraíba and the Paulista plateau showed contrasting responses to the sequence of socioeconomic polarizations. In the first case, the *senhor* struggled with adversity with no possibility of winning; in the second, the *senhor* undertook a kind of agricultural revolution that kept everything of value in the archaic structures of the great plantations, yet set out to prune them of everything not serving the ends of production, as if to impose a kind of "economic rationalization" on slave labor. Both cases clearly display the position of struggle that informed the human actor's understanding and projection of the social use of competition. The forces that could crush him were beyond his reach; nothing he might do could modify their nature or their fatal course. Nevertheless, their consequences, which in the final analysis were what concerned the *senhor*, could be manipulated, and by means that were within his reach (owing to his key position in the structure of national society and to the power he derived from that position).

Clearly, such a social perspective necessarily led to images and social uses of competition that were distorted. From the *senhor's* world view, economic realism did not lead to a secularized and "rational" perception of competition, seen in terms of the dynamic equilibrium of the market, but to a *cataclysmic conception of economic forces*. Since the personal security of the actor and the success of his undertakings were couched in terms of this conception, it ultimately gave rise to a typical form of economic privatism. This was the sort of "modern" private initiative that flourished in a society of castes and estates. It was merely the cultural objectification of estate criteria concerning the organization of power and a conception of the world. For the privileged economic actor in a slave economy it was natural to make his key position a privileged position and to use it as a shield against economic risks. However, in doing so he was incorporating his own condition as a capitalist economic actor into a social structure that was extra- and anticapitalist. "Free initiative" and "private enterprise" were transformed into the privileges of estate, to be respected and protected above and beyond any rationality inherent in the economic processes in the narrow sense.

Therefore, historically, competition emerged with two faces. On the one hand it enhanced many times over the privileged economic actor's power to act; yet at the same time it was destructive of society's overall economic equilibrium. Society had to suffer all the manipulations that sustained and fomented the "economic privatism" we have described. Exchange rates, tariffs, price policies (directed toward the internal market to guarantee low costs for certain goods, or toward the external market to attempt to guarantee rates of profit), credit policies, sales taxes, as well as other expedients, all had the same purpose. The general public bore the risks and supported, directly and indirectly, the position of the privileged economic actor. Thus competition was not led into those socially constructive channels which in advanced capitalist societies linked together private property, free enterprise, and the redistribution of income and power. It was quickly redefined— economically, socially, and politically—as an aspect of the distribution of income and power within the estates, and hence of severe concentration of income and power. For this reason, these mechanisms did not give rise to structural shifts of income and power. Such was not the latent function of competition. It became what it had to become within the context of an exporting colonial economy based on slavery, and in a dependent developing capitalist economy: namely, the means by which society protected its one main source of production and wealth through the position of its privileged economic agents.[2]

The second type of tension, born of discrepancies between "attributed status" and "real status" in the middling ranks, has not yet been studied with regard to imperial society. Indeed, with the knowledge we now have it is not easy to reduce its various facets to a common denominator (especially if one takes into account the rising social groups such as the importers, wholesale merchants, the middlemen in the import and export business, etc). The paradigm, of course (for the purposes of sociological analysis as well as historically), was the member of the "traditional" or "grand families" who belonged to civil society but did not enjoy seigneurial status in the strict sense. By virtue of occupations, alliances, and social level, such persons embraced and were embraced by the dominant estates for traditional as well as for specifically "modern" reasons. Indeed, whether through individual talents or because of needs arising from the fusion of patrimonialism with the bureaucracy, they even succeeded in entering into the economic, social, and political elite of these estates (acting, however, in accordance with their own interests and values within the structures of power). Whether "liberals" or "conservatives" (or even "republicans"), they owed their loyalty in practical affairs to these interests and values and to the traditional code of honor.

The origins of those social circles that were conventionally the most respected and prestigious of the estates is a question of major importance in this analysis. At the turn from the eighteenth to the nineteenth century they were lost in the mists of tradition, which equated formally the various branches of the "traditional grand families." The legitimate members of a seigneurial family, rural or urban, enjoyed roughly the same status, at least in their self-estimation and in their intercourse with peers, plebeians, slaves, and freedmen. However, the absorption of seigneurial domination by the establishment set off a process of differentiation, perceptible from the beginning, of status and social roles. Because of the privileges invested in seigneurial position, political power flowed into the hands of those who in fact possessed supreme authority within the patriarchal family and patrimonial domination. This differentiation intensified, and in the course of time was normalized as a structural and dynamic requisite of the social and political organization of national society. As a consequence, within the establishment, incorporated into civil society, only one rank possessed all the power and performed hegemonic functions. The others—even those who shielded themselves behind the mists of tradition and the fictions of nobility and equality—were either lesser partners in the distribution of power or had no power at all, as was the case with the *homens livres** of the populace.

Nevertheless, the "modern" requirements of the expanding market economy and the independent state moved the intermediate ranks into top positions in a variety of occupations—politics, business, public administration, liberal professions, journalism, education, military professions, etc.—and into the social arena where the elite was chosen. This mobility not only served as a counterweight and supplement to prestige, it also brought certain sectors of the middling ranks into contact with the exercise of power, on the basis of the traditionalist mechanisms of loyalty to one's estate and familial-patriarchal solidarity. This did not introduce equality among the various social levels, nor did it undermine stratification within the estates, inasmuch as the entire process of differentiation and readjustment took place out of the very need to preserve this type of stratification within a "national order." Nonetheless,

---

*The expression *"homem(ns) livre(s)"*—"free men"—refers to that social group which possessed only enough property to provide subsistence, or slightly more. They were nearly always quite dependent on the rural aristocracy for the guarantee of their land titles, and in return they pledged their votes, which they were eligible, as property owners, to cast. They were also mobilized as private armies, when necessary.—Ed.

they did breathe new life into the social fictions that sustained outmoded ideas of the social status and the social roles of the "well-born," and in addition gave new dimensions to the functioning and to the political implications of these statuses and roles. In any situation, but especially in situations that were likely to involve their social prestige, the members of the middling ranks hoped to be treated, and to be able to act socially, as members of the dominant ranks (as if the specific weight attached to the seigneurial condition within the establishment had no relevance for them). But this changed the historical reality not at all. Those who possessed the power derived from the seigneurial condition accepted in good faith this fictitious equality, nourished by tradition and patrimonialist solidarity through the bonds of kinship and vassalage, through a provincial code of honor, etc., and derived enormous practical advantage from it, since in this way the hegemonic ranks bound to themselves the middling ranks, who entertained no likelihood of achieving autonomy or of "rebellion within the established order." Consequently, these distinctions, with their linkages to power, had no effect whatsoever on the normal functioning of the *status quo*. On the contrary, they strengthened it, mobilizing and facilitating identities of interests and social loyalties that otherwise would not have been so useful to the consolidation of the existing order. Only the slave and the freedman caused any real friction, which irked "persons of good conduct" without, however, upsetting the material, juridical, and political foundations of national society. There remained no more than the relative frustration of the middling ranks, who engaged in a muted struggle to salvage lost social position and the appearances of "equality with the top" through compensatory attitudes and behaviors.[3]

In this material, emotional, and moral situation, the middling ranks were also compelled to go beyond the limits (and at times even the standards) of the forms of personal or group competition sanctioned by convention and tradition. For them, however, the risks and hazards that were to be confronted were situated within the very society in which they lived. These risks and hazards were not manifested in the persons or the actions of the real "wielders of power." Rather, the commotions of the social order, which affected the relative social position of the middling ranks, constantly threatening their social status, were what they perceived as their historical nightmare. At stake here, with fatal and even cataclysmic import, was the access of these ranks to the privileges of a social order of castes and estates based on slavery and seigneurial domination, rendered more complex and effective after independence by the fusion of patrimonial and bureaucratic domination. The preservation of their share of privilege, in the course of tumultuous events and massive historical transformations, became the principal psychological, social, and political goal of the most active circles of the middling ranks. During the first quarter of the nineteenth century, this goal was never a real problem. However, after the consolidation of the regime, the gap within the ranks of civil society began to grow, aggravated by a new factor. The growth of the urban economy and of the agricultural frontier raised persons of "inferior social extraction"—about whom it could not always be said that they "stemmed from the best branches"—into the upper echelons, and hence also to honors and the nobility.*[4] Under such circumstances privilege appeared as more than just a social value. It served as a barometer that gauged the oscillations of social groups within the historical process. The middling ranks concentrated on an obstinate defense of privileges that they felt were theirs by right or they were loathe to lose.

Consequently, the members of these ranks frequently found themselves compelled to make social use of competition in ways that diverged from conventional models. They could do this because they were protected by certain advantages conferred upon them by the roles they occupied in politics, administration, business, liberal professions, education, the military, journalism, etc. These roles enabled them to adapt various aspects of the legal order to the interests and convenience of their own rank. Through various subterfuges, the modernization of legislation, policy, and administration served, in fact, the latent function of offsetting their relative loss of social prestige by evening out economic, social, and political privileges. The effect of this was the emergence of useful, outwardly "democratic" innovations. Thus these ranks transferred to the general public the burden of financing their own status—something no longer within their own means—through measures such as free education and other social benefits to which the general public would not have easy access. But this also had a paradoxical result. The stoutest defenders of the privileged order were actually not the "most privileged." The "junior partners," who

---

*Brazil during the Empire created a life-time nobility, several knightly orders, honorary ranks in the national guard, and other signs of royal favor.—Ed.

fulfilled innovative and occasionally even revolutionary functions, all the while jealously safeguarded the nucleus of the *status quo*.

This structural and dynamic reworking of competition into a social force is fundamental. It shows how the slavocratic and seigneurial social order deformed the process, linking it in a clear-cut and decisive manner to an ultraconservative and terrifically egoistic context for the absorption of social unrest and inescapable institutional innovations. From this perspective, the privatism of the middling ranks provided a counterpoint to the seigneurial rank. This took objective social form, as if the private interests of groups that were able to get their hands on "private property" and carry on "free enterprise" were the true altar of the Fatherland. All was owed to them "in the nature of things." This psychocultural link-up of competition became a socially constructive influence for the evolution of national society only when the disintegration of the seigneurial order had reached its climax. Then the discrepancies between the "attributed" and "real" status of the middling ranks, though not the spark, were fuel added to the fire. The resentments and frustrations at last found a channel that led to an astonishing reorientation of attitudes and conduct. Nonetheless, once they had passed the crisis and the euphoria that had led them at the last moment to support the fall of the monarchy and the establishment of the Republic, these ranks returned to their former routine. They continued to cling—now as an "emergent middle class"—to modernization and democratization as mere expedients for ensuring privileged treatment of their interests and their social destiny. They never desired for even a moment a revolution within the system or the reign of the sort of equality such as that consecrated by the competitive social order, since they remained at bottom prisoners of the *ancien régime*, even while struggling against its superficial features and its internal ranking. They delivered themselves to an obscure historical mission, guardians of the perpetuation of "conservative power" and of the most hated privilege of rank, which had survived the disappearance of both colonial and imperial society.

The third kind of tension, that of value conflict between ideal norms and practical norms guiding the social roles of the *senhor*, has been abundantly studied by scholars. Indeed, any society that clashes head-on with its value system is vulnerable to this kind of conflict. The forms of socialization, situations of interest, and indirect social controls are able to neutralize this kind of

tension (in the process widening, of course, the need for conformity, given this weakness), at least to the extent that the social
order that gave rise to it possesses mechanisms of self-defense and
self-preservation. This does not prevent the continual eruption of
crises of conscience nor certain modalities of nonconformism
which, though condemning inconsistencies within the value system,
nonetheless accept the foundations of the established order. As a
rule, as Pareto has pointed out in a brilliant analysis, the spokesmen of nonconformity stem from the dominant strata and its
elites. Their criticism derives from such a strong, pure, and fanatical identification with the ideal mores and values neglected or betrayed in daily practice that in the end it pours over into specifically revolutionary forms of transformation of the system. The
simplest example of opposition of this sort—which is couched in
moral terms and hence contains its own justification—occurs in
the case of the "moral revolution." A more complicated example
is linked to utopian protest, which finds its own *raison d'être* in the
existing social order. The moral revolution was of broad significance within the sociohistorical context of national liberation. It
set into motion in the history of national society a number of
trends in various directions, since it was only after political emancipation that the social and economic order of castes and estates
inherited from the colony was finally able to realize its own potential for differentiation and development. But this revolution ended,
turning on its own axes, exhausting the "revolution within the traditional order" without going beyond the bounds of seigneurial interests. On the historical scene, no social groups or strata emerged
intent on galvanizing the "moral revolution" in directions that
might have brought about the negation and destruction of the
slavocratic and seigneurial order, the movements of this sort that
did occur being local, weak, and episodic. The middling ranks,
which should have provided the leadership cadres for an insurgency
of this sort, identified materially and morally (and hence politically) with the militant defense of the *status quo*. Despite the
strong pressures to conform deriving from the traditional and autocratic patterns of seigneurial rule, the social order based on castes
and estates showed cracks nonetheless, and was open to the manifestation of an increasingly stronger moral rebellion with utopian
underpinnings. Moreover, it was not the estate and caste structure
of society but rather the inconsistencies attendant on the status of
the citizen that became the focal point of differences. These in-

consistencies were, in fact, the major obstacle to the formation of an authentic national society (indeed, how could such a society be formed, given the existence not only of slaves and freedmen but also, of "free men" who were systematically excluded from the legal order?). The predominance of seigneurial interests and the social hegemony of the rural aristocracy nonetheless served to obfuscate the revolutionary fulcrum of the Brazilian national dilemma. While the retention of slavery was upheld as a "general necessity," at the same time there was agitation for a "renewal of the social order" on the basis of the *status quo* (not on the basis of what the civil society of a nation ought to be). As a result, slavery became the natural point of convergence for any open or veiled manifestation of utopian protest. It offended religious mores, the "rights of a civilized people," and the ideal requisites of the legal order, while its suppression would provide the obvious basis for the further expansion of capitalism. That is why the "defense of the established order" (i.e., those who accepted and approved of slavery, negating the reigning value system) as well as "the revolution within the system" (i.e., those who demanded the abolition of slavery, believing that they were affirming the existing value system, although they advocated neither the elimination of white supremacy nor equality between the "races") both organized spontaneously around the issue of slavery.

Here we shall discuss only those implications of this value conflict that had bearing on the social use of competition by members of the seigneurial and middling ranks. By the very nature of this dissidence, it was to appear prematurely in the words and deeds of exemplary figures. As such, however, it was born and died as an isolated phenomenon, with no repercussions. The equilibrium of the slavocratic and seigneurial order had to be upset at some fundamental point for the debate to make its appearance on the historical scene as a social movement. When this happened, the protagonists of the differing social currents were compelled to express, at least hypothetically, the most radical and advanced forms of liberal thought. It might have been expected that they would in some way embody refined and complex tendencies of utopian protest. However, this did not happen. Led to its ultimate consequences by the disintegration of the regime, utopian protest acquired an unexpected revolutionary breadth and then undermined, along with slavery, the estate basis of the organization of the economy, of society, and of power. This result dismayed even Nabuco,* the paladin of Brazilian liberalism, showing that he himself had not intended to go so far and that abolitionism, as a social movement, had been transcended by concrete history. Utopian protest, therefore, turned the wheel of history, availing itself of the link between the release of repressed forces of social change and the transformation of the structures of power, without, however, directly provoking or determining either. On the contrary, the champions of abolitionism, with few exceptions, rejected the historical mission they embodied, above all the consequent "bourgeois explosion." On the other hand, the abolitionists who rejected simultaneously slavery and the seigneurial order—as for example, the São Paulo Republicans—held themselves back. They had foreseen this explosion" and where it would lead: to the destruction of the entire framework of imperial society and the transition to a new social order.

Indeed, the purest and most creative competitive action in the old slavocratic and seigneurial social order is without a doubt to be found in the behavioral inclinations and ideals of the utopian dissidents. This action centered on impersonal motives and consciously endeavored to avoid at all costs the eruption of violence and conflict (which could have gone "too far," giving rise to uncontrollable situations and the appearance of rebellious popular masses, or even "race war"). Further, their social goal, at the very least incongruous and anachronistic, was to increase the flexibility of the existing social order, adapting it to the material and formal needs of capitalism. These impulses were not enough to bring about a more thorough and profound sociocultural elaboration of either the idea or the uses of competition. The reason for this appears to derive from two circumstances, both extraneous to the abolitionist message. First, there was the very nature of utopian tension, self-contained, undertaking a "moral revolution," "within the system." As a consequence, abolitionism was limited both ideologically and politically by the conventionalism inherent in the general cultural horizon of seigneurial circles. Competition was exploited skillfully and effectively, but without opening up any true alternative to the

---

*Joaquim Nabuco (1849-1910), known especially as an abolitionist. See his *Abolitionism: The Brazilian Antislavery Struggle*, trans. Robert Conrad (Urbana, Ill., 1977).—Ed.

cooperation imposed by patrimonialist solidarity and a bestowed freedom, the two poles of "seigneurial ethics." There was no attempt to bridge the gulf that in the end opened up and was astutely exploited by a spontaneous alliance of Republican "realists," ultra-radical circles of the middling ranks, and the most enlightened businessmen (in the coffee industry and the urban commercial economy). Second, there was the elite cast of mind that ever presided over abolitionism. Those who accept a mandate that is not expressly delegated, however purely they may go about fulfilling their mission, surely belong on a social level with the oppressors. However genuine their utopian inspirations may be, they never transcend the human condition of the actor. Indeed, this was brought out quite clearly. Once the period of feverish agitation was past, there were few (Antonio Bento was the best example) who continued, teeth clenched, to combat the final spoliation of the slave, made possible by abolition itself, fraternizing with the negro and the mulatto as human beings. It was evident that for the majority, abolitionism began and ended with the historical concerns of the rich and powerful white. He had to destroy slavery in order to have done once and for all with the shackles imposed by the slavocratic and seigneurial order on the internal expansion of capitalism (in other words, to establish new conditions for economic, social, and political development).

The revolutionary nexus enables us to get to the root of the problem. In a society of estates, competition is restrained not only when differences in social level exist. It cannot be exercised freely, even in "relations among equals," without jeopardizing the very foundations of social equilibrium and the continued existence of the social order. These considerations explain certain inclinations, so deep-rooted among the elites of imperial society, toward trying to keep competitive relationships within the framework of a gentlemen's agreement. Since such relationships seemed an explosive element, it was sought to localize and discipline competition socially to prevent the forms of seigneurial control from losing their effectiveness. Society was shielded from the corrosive "bourgeois spirit," and men's bonds were strengthened—to their social levels, to their corresponding codes of honor, and to the myth that Brazil was ungovernable without some autocratic-paternalist version of enlightened despotism. The slave-master relationship and seigneurial rule thus undermined the psychological foundations of moral and political life, making the social individuation of the person, or the transformation of the "individual," "individual will," and "personal freedom" into the psychodynamic and sociodynamic underpinnings of social life a very difficult and precarious process. Is there any need to point out that in the seigneurial cosmos the only kind of individualism that could exist was that arising from the exacerbated will of the master and imposing its authority from top down? This cosmos was closed not only to the other kind of individualism, which requires the interchange between "equal wills" as much as between "unequal wills"; within it even this individualism was confused with the glorification of anarchy and with the downfall of "civilized life."

It may be concluded from this discussion that the structural-functional inconsistencies of the system of status and social roles of the dominant ranks subjected the slavocratic seigneurial order to diverse tensions, permitting competition to be absorbed in ways that clashed with cultural tradition. One might say that that social order contained certain breaches through which the bourgeois spirit infiltrated, in time undermining the foundations of social equilibrium.[5] Nonetheless, the slavocratic and seigneurial social order for a long time withstood the impact of tensions generated by these discrepancies; it was able for a long time to shield itself from the disintegration that was bound to ensue from the differentiation of the capitalist elements that were a part of that order, and from the irradiation of urban markets and the internal expansion of capitalism. Resistance was weakened by the setbacks suffered by slavery—the prohibition of the slave traffic, and later the emancipation laws.* Nonetheless, competition was absorbed, emerging as a social process in various situations that became central to the development of a "modern" urban style of life. As it grew it would not only come to function as a social force incompatible with the equilibrium and perpetuation of the slavocratic seigneurial order; it would also prove to be an uncontrollable sociodynamic influence, which would undermine estate criteria for the attribution of status and social roles, of economic or political solidarity, etc., and accelerate the disintegration of the dominant estates. Thus the disintegration and downfall of the Brazilian seigneurial regime may be explained in part as a kind of explosion of tensions that had ac-

---

*The slave traffic was effectively outlawed in 1850. Children born of slaves after 1871 were declared free in that year; sexagenarians were freed in 1885; and final abolition came in 1888. —Ed.

cumulated on account of the estate and caste structure of society, especially at the summit, in the seigneurial and middling ranks. Hence, contrary to what is believed, it was not only the crisis of slave labor which destroyed the equilibrium of the seigneurial world. It was also undermined from within. The crisis of slave labor, seen from this perspective, constituted the inexorable element that prevented any resolution of the deeper tensions by means of a "revolution within the established order" (or any solution that would enable these tensions to be resolved and overcome, keeping the seigneurial order intact).

On the other hand, the same conclusions suggest that during the sociohistorical process described, competition was assimilated (albeit fragmentarily and but partially) by the slavocratic and seigneurial order itself, where it became a secondary but active influence. In its more remote origins it was linked with the interests, social values, and lifestyle of the privileged and dominant estates. In terms of the ideal requisites, the integration and functioning of what would later become the competitive social order, this development may be seen sociologically as the source of a deformation. Serving as a factor in the retention or revitalization of estate privileges, competition became linked (genetically, structurally, and functionally) to processes that inhibited and interfered with the development of the class system, or sustained indefinitely behavioral patterns and patterns of social relationships that were variously precapitalist and anticapitalist. The situation was ambiguous, since we now see the opposite side of the coin: incorporated into relatively archaic sociohistorical or sociocultural contexts, the dynamic social factors engendered by competition contributed to maintaining or preserving "the past in the present," strengthening rather than destroying archaic elements in the process. This state of things is truly important, even though it has not been well studied. It seems to be one of the reasons for the feeble capacity of the class system to drive capitalist economic development onward. The cultural horizon steers capitalist economic behavior more toward the acquisition of privilege (in the old style) than toward the conquest of autonomous economic, social, and political power, which explains the identification with dependent capitalism and the persistence of semicolonial (actually either precapitalist or subcapitalist) economic complexes. We must underscore especially the close links that were established as capitalism developed, between substantially conservative (or, in other terms, particularist and elitist) social interests and values and the shaping of the competitive social order. In its historical, economic, and political roots, that order bound the present to the past as an iron chain. In one historical period competition may have accelerated the decline and collapse of caste and estate society; later, however, it chained capitalist expansion to a crude, rigidly particularist and fundamentally autocratic privatism, as if the "modern bourgeois" had emerged from the ashes of the "old *senhor*." In other words, it engendered a social order in which privilege, in addition to class inequality, weighs heavily in the universalization of competition as a social relation and social process. The competitive social order that resulted is therefore not very aggressive in breaking down the barriers to the expansion of the class system, and very moderate as regards the spread and imposition of new patterns of class relations, as if "bourgeois rationality" were feared and the anticompetitive values of the old seigneurial world ought to be harbored forever.

The other disintegrating influence, specifically important for the elaboration of competition as a sociocultural factor, was the reorganization and development of the urban economy, toward which the slavocratic and seignorial order displayed a lack of flexibility. What we may call the "new sector" of the economy had two opposing dynamic aspects within the context of political emancipation and the formation of national society. On the one hand it appeared as a natural outgrowth of population increase and tendencies toward urban concentration, at least in the capital of the country and in some of the large cities of the period. On the other hand, in the form it took and in the functions it performed in the reintegration of the Brazilian economy into the world economy, it represented a forward bastion for economic dynamics controlled by the hegemonic centers of the world economy. In this respect the new sector developed into a kind of satellite market organized as a specialized consumer economy, capturing a part of the economic surplus that might have been absorbed by the hegemonic centers (through the exportation of finished goods and the direct or indirect control of internal commerce). The slavocratic and seigneurial order at first was able to adapt to this development, especially as long as the old pattern of relative autonomy in large-scale agricultural production was maintained and the cities did not grow so large as to affect the foundations of traditional patrimonial and bureaucratic rule of the dominant estates. Since change in this domain took place slowly, there existed economic, social, and political foundations favorable to the absorption of the new sector by the slavocratic and seigneurial order. Nonetheless, because of the nature of external economic interests and the scale on which they took over key positions in the internal market, through the institutional reorganization of the entire export and import trade, what emerged in the city was a modern-appearing capitalist market (adapted to the conditions of the country and to the satellite functions it was obliged to perform). The slavocratic and seigneurial social order had no way to absorb it. Instead it would gradually be absorbed by it: first, through transactions in which the economic surplus from agricultural production was in fact channeled into trade and into the world of urban business; second, by the growing specialization of the great plantations in the crop-growing and livestock economy, which led the *senhor* to purchase food and other items of use on the domestic market; and finally, by the shift some of them made to producing partially (and in some areas and in certain sectors totally) for this market. As free wage labor, i.e., the labor market became universal—indeed, even while slavery still existed the structure and equilibrium of these production units began to be affected by it—this process of absorption achieved full circle. Indeed, this process was part of the "very logic of the situation," and in the end the economic system that was to emerge in the cities proved to be the more complex and advanced system, notwithstanding any differentiation, structural or functional, that might occur (but only did occur in the east of São Paulo, and then only as a transitory phenomenon) in the slavocratic and seigneurial system of production, and ultimately came to prevail over the latter (eroding the foundations of its autonomy and its dominant position).

Thus, in spite of the social and political hegemony of seigneurial interests, or of their fundamental significance for the growth of the urban economy, they proved incapable of absorbing or regulating, either structurally or dynamically, the economic processes that the urban economy had set into motion (or for which it had opened the door through a policy of attracting "strong" and "specialized" economic actors from outside). The expansion of the new sector was relatively chaotic and undirected, and only a few of its various phases and effects could be controlled effectively from inside the economy, in accordance with the criteria or interests of the existing social order. The situation created the appearance of a bustling "economic freedom" and an upsurge of "free enterprise" in the business world. Behind the facade, however, there was an uncontrolled freedom, typical of the emergence of the capitalist market in colonial economies in transformation. Society did not have the means to contain and regulate the economic actors; it had gradually to forge them, frequently above and beyond the material, moral, and political bounds of the existing social order. Against this background, however, it was still that order which prevented the economy from being crushed, and the reestablishment of a full-fledged colonial state. It turned out that the existence of a rural aristocracy, armed politically with the power of society and the state, proved to be an appreciable restraint on the upsurge of external economic interests, in particular their manifestations in the urban sector. Ventures essential to the shaping of a capitalist market economy, which appeared and indeed were "imperative," collided with the systematic or "reactionary" resistance (both open and covert) of the dominant ranks, who thus tried to gain some control over the wide-ranging process of modernization of the means of trade, communication, and transport. A situation of potential political conflict therefore took shape. Those who defended rapid and intensive institutional modernization of the economy closed their eyes or tacitly accepted the risks attendant on a greater external control over the internal economy, direct or indirect. Those who adamantly opposed any modernization defended the *status quo* within the limits of exclusive seigneurial privilege. Between the two extremes, there prevailed an accommodation (fashioned, of course, by the "conservative" wing of seigneurial interests) which championed a kind of bargaining posture, both conscious and deliberate. This was focused on two converging ends: (1) to contain outside dependence (or subordination to visible external domination) within predominantly economic and technical domains; (2) to prevent the organization and growth of the modern internal capitalist market from neutralizing the economic advantages deriving from the establishment of a national state and producing a disguised latter-day imitation of the hated "colonial pact."

With the power structures preserved, the forces of accommodation prevailed down the line, inhibiting or frustrating attempts to adapt the internal market to the interests, pure and simple, of the world economy, which were threatening (or appeared to threaten) "national independence." External pressure had to find appropriate means to impose its influence. It was not concerned with the degree of flexibility in the mechanisms of the domestic market, but with the kind of control it hoped to exercise over them (from either within or without: the placement of the controls was not so important for firms that dominated both ends of the "economic position"). External pressures concentrated on that element on which the equilibrium and continued existence of the seigneurial order were materially dependent: slavery and the replenishment of slave labor. By cutting off the supply of slaves, it smothered, in the long run, the slavocratic and seigneurial order, at the cost of conflicts that did not, at the time, manifest what exactly was at stake economically and politically.* Feeling their status threatened (since the *senhores* were not blind to the consequences of this subtle operation), the ruling ranks demanded from their elites a firm political direction that would transform the "agricultural sector" into a true bastion of the regime. The central problems of the organization and growth of the domestic market on wholly capitalist foundations were therefore not overlooked because of incompetence or negligence (as is supposed by those who interpret the "Mauá failure"—or the spirit that he embodied—in too strict or short-sighted terms).** These problems came up against a reaction that was impassive, although obdurate. This the ministries, both conservative and liberal, had to cope with in order to "maintain civil peace." The crown's Moderating Power [right to call new ministries or elections] merely ensured, from its position above party politics, that the static limits of the system were not seriously threatened. Following this interpretation, the impassivity and obduracy were not dictated merely by traditionalist (as some would have it) or nationalist (as others would have it) motives. They were part of a systematic defense, broadly and deeply conscious, of the economic and power structures that the seigneurial strata and their elites considered seriously endangered—not by the world market in itself, but because of the appearance of an internal market intricately meshed with the world market and broadly determined by forces that in time would no longer be controllable by the extensions of the power of the rural aristoc-

---

*This passage refers to the British campaign to stop the African slave traffic. These efforts began while Brazil was still a colony, and climaxed in the late 1840s with captures of slave ships within sight of Rio de Janeiro.—Ed.

**The Viscount Mauá was the most outstanding entrepreneur during the Empire. His eventual bankruptcy has been variously explained by historians.—Ed.

racy. In this sense, the lack of flexibility in the slavocratic and seigneurial order in face of the upsurge of capitalism as an internal economic reality above all expressed a specific reaction of self-defense. This market was to grow and in turn provide the basis for the economic and social reclassification of the existing strata, destroying by its very existence the classificatory functions of the slavocratic and seigneurial order, and engendering, materially and dynamically, a class system. This took place, not because of the inaction of the seigneurial estates and their elites, but because they were unable to stop history: opting for political emancipation, they had chosen capitalism as the alternative to the "infamous colonial pact" and were obliged to resign themselves to the destiny (and its shocks) which that choice had in store for them.

It can be seen that the seigneurial estates tried to establish a certain consensus with regard to the institutional modernization of the economy and to the pace of internal expansion of the capitalist market, in direct relation to their economic interests (which were far from homogeneous) and in inverse relation to the foreseeable social and political risks (which did attain considerable homogeneity). They undertook, simultaneously, (1) a persistent and thoroughgoing defense of the slavocratic and seigneurial social order, upon which the continuity and effectiveness of the socioeconomic forms elaborated during the colonial period depended; (2) an uncompromising rejection of the functions of the capitalist market as a means for defining the social worth and social class of human groupings hitherto kept at the "margin of society and history." The economic success of the seigneurial estates was a function of social and political structures. Only that which was destined for the world market, and that which was bought from the slave dealer, passed through the market. The structure of society otherwise had nothing to do with the functions of the market, which did not operate as an agency of social classification. The incorporation of a kind of market that would perform such functions seemed predestined to destroy "social peace," introducing, together with a free labor market, other criteria of social classification (or declassification), and rendering, as time passed, the noneconomical guarantees of "economic success" much more complex and uncertain. A capitalist market creates economic structures from which none can escape and a society in which everyone must respond to the same rules, from those concerning relations of production to those concerning the relations of power. Hence if the seigneurial and slavocratic social order did not bend to the requirements and conditions of a capitalist market, it was, at bottom, because of a genuine impossibility of absorbing the material, moral, and political forms of human relations such as exist in a capitalist economy. Competition, as a process structurally and dynamically determined by relations among persons and social groups in the market, was incompatible with the patrimonialist foundations of social life and with estate criteria of social classification and declassification. For this reason, the seigneurial estates and their elites showed themselves to be open to insitutional modernization of the economy at levels on which economic structures of the existing social order were at one and the same time adapted to capital and were not adversely affected by it (i.e., at a level where the *senhor* could perform capitalist economic functions and where the internal economic process was determined by the organization of the world market). At other levels, a negative and resistant aspect was to prevail, of selective reaction and mistrustful filtering of the institutional modernization of the internal economy. In consequence, the internal expansion of the capitalist market initially (until the last quarter of the nineteenth century) followed the rhythms and fluctuations of the disintegration of the slavocratic and seigneurial social order. They also reflect how the new competitive social order emerged step by step in this difficult birth of a "bourgeois style of life." The specifically capitalist element in the previous order did not at all facilitate this transition; on the contrary, it served as an obstacle imposed economically as well as socially and politically "from the top down."[6]

A tension thus formed which affected the pattern of integration and equilibrium of the national society. The established social order could not adapt without decomposing—destroying itself in the process—into the economic forms emerging from direct incorporation into the world market and from assimilation of economic institutions that were to regulate the organization, functioning, and growth of the internal market in accordance with universal, specifically capitalist patterns. At the beginning, the tension was easily diluted and neutralized, despite aggravating external pressures that were driving it toward eruption. A colonial economy is not very sensitive to such pressures, if protected by a stable social system in which power is autocratically organized (of course, "centralized from within"). Under such conditions, it is almost impossible to foment by such means a crisis deep enough to sweep away the social and political foundations of the established order. Nonetheless, the apparent security, an outgrowth of social stability and the rigorous use of power, helped to bring about what the external pressures by themselves could not: a kind of chronic and dogged blindness, inducing the helmsman himself to steer the ship toward the abyss. In the Brazilian case, this rule proved itself in an exemplary manner. Even with slavery and seigneurial rule preserved inviolable, a number of pathways opened up that would have enabled the existing social regime to adapt to integration into the world market as well as to the internal expansion of the specifically capitalist and predominantly urban and commercial "new sector." This was, moreover, the logical road for the country to take in preparing itself for the transition from colonial economic forms to capitalist economic forms. Nonetheless, the seigneurial estates and their elites were blind to it, being fascinated instead by the specious security of the slavocratic and seigneurial order and by the autocratic power it gave them. This provides a sociological explanation for the drastic and deliberate reduction of the field of political action of these estates and their elites, who through their ambitions, lifestyle, and an increasingly inappropriate ideology almost totally paralyzed their own capacity to make decisions and direct events. Indeed, not a few members of the ruling estates (or those close to them by dint of economic interest and political loyalty) perceived the real meaning of the crisis in all currents of political thought. Rarely, however, even taking into account leading party and political figures, did their ideas or beliefs pass through the selective screen of "public opinion," the ultraconservative consensus of the ruling estates (seigneurial or not). This was done only in relatively noncontroversial matters of common interest within these circles, or in matters requiring a minimum of deliberate innovations and susceptible to effective direct or indirect control (and hence threatening to the equilibrium of the seigneurial slavocratic order).

This all-embracing mechanism proved to be quite useful and efficient over both the short and middle term, ensuring the dominant estates an obvious political success that enabled them to retain as much as possible of the colonial order in their own hands through the perpetuation of slavery and seigneurial domination. They were also able to preserve, along with "internal order," the territorial, economic, and social unity of the country. However, on a broader scale, and over the long term, the same mechanism had an injurious effect, since it rendered the seigneurial ranks and their elites powerless to confront and contain the storm when it was finally unleashed by internal pressures. In the first place, the absence of a conscious and intelligent effort to coordinate and steer the emergent economic forces left the slavocratic and seigneurial order stripped of its ability to struggle for its survival over the long term. It could adapt neither structurally nor dynamically to the exercise of control of the new economic order forming and growing in the urban sector, either in accordance with its own interests or in accordance with the social, political, and economic requirements of an internal market resting on specifically capitalist foundations.[7] The forces of this new economic order burst forth and grew spontaneously and chaotically, with lethal effect on slavery and seigneurial domination. They undermined and destroyed the "old social order," which did not try to understand, absorb, or control them while a reconciliation between past and future was still possible. Second, the absence of a conscious and intelligent effort to coordinate and steer the emergent economic forces prevented the long period of survival of the slavocratic and seigneurial order from acting constructively to prepare the economy for the coming need for total commercialization of all levels and phases of the national system. The result was a kind of differential adaptation of economic behavior that enabled the privileged economic actor of the seigneurial and slavocratic order to monopolize the advantages deriving at one and the same time from the preservation of noncapitalist economic structures of slave-based production and from the initial unfolding of the new economic sector. This duality could not be maintained indefinitely without more profound dynamic and structural adaptations. It stimulated a "parallelism in economic growth" wherein everything went well for the dominant estates as long as the slavocratic and seigneurial foundations of the existing order were able to guarantee this monopolistic position. Clearly, as soon as this condition broke down, nothing could save the seigneurial and slavocratic order. The dominant ranks found themselves condemned to bring the destruction of that order to completion with their own hands in order to salvage the social and political privileges attendant on their economic situation. This is what happened when the "crisis of slave labor" entered its acute phase, carrying with it the slavocratic and seigneurial order (but not its social and political substrate, the oligarchic basis of the autocratic power of the "rich" and "privileged").

It is safe to conclude, on the basis of sociological analysis, that the lack of flexibility shown by the slavocratic and seigneurial social order when faced with the emergence and expansion of capitalism as an internal historical reality gave rise to a temporary accommodation of opposing and mutually exclusive economic forms. This accommodation produced a "national" hybrid economy that promoted the coexistence and interpenetration of economic forms, variously "archaic" and "modern," by dint of which the economic system adapted itself to the structures and functions of a differentiated albeit peripheral and dependent capitalist economy (since only dependent capitalism permits and requires such a combination of the "modern" with the "archaic"—a *minimum of decolonization* with a *maximum of modernization*). This accommodation may be seen as both "historically necessary" and "economically useful." It extended the limits of survival of a precapitalist system of production, which was able to seal off, partially or totally, farming, ranching, and mining from the encroachment of the free labor market, all the while that an internal capitalist market (and hence a capitalist labor market) was in full flower and expanding apace. This same accommodation established conditions for the urban commercial sector to expand and differentiate slowly but surely, although it deprived it of the stimulus to growth it would have received from the rapid mercantilization of relations of production in the countryside and from the universal establishment of market relations on a national scale. Finally, this accommodation established a steady flow of profit, which favored the growth and dynamic use of the economic surplus, linking together the "ultramodern" and the "ultra-archaic" structurally and dynamically in a state of mutual coexistence. These three developments are fundamental to the emergence of *modern Brazil*, regardless of how any one of them, or all taken together jointly, might be assessed sociologically. Nonetheless, the accommodation described did not bring about, nor could it have, a reconciliation between preexisting economic structures based on slave labor, semi-servile labor, and patrimonial domination, on the one hand, and the emergent economic structures, based on free labor and on specifically capitalist forms of production and exchange, on the other. As a consequence, in the overall historical context, they fulfilled distinct social functions that were potentially in conflict. The former contributed to maintaining the existence of the slavocratic and seigneurial order and to reducing the pace of decolonization, creating structural and dynamic conditions that prevented the development of a full-fledged capitalist economic system. The latter tended to isolate and eliminate "archaic" economic forms and to consolidate free labor at various levels of social life, a process that at one and the same time transformed them into an element serving to dissolve the slavocratic and seigneurial social order, while acting as a progressive factor in unifying the economic system on capitalist foundations.

To sum up, by provoking the emergence of a truly capitalist market, albeit one with limited forms and functions, the changed relationship with the world market forced the slavocratic and seigneurial social order to fuel a kind of economic growth that transcended and negated preexisting economic structures. Nonetheless, over the short and middle terms the economic growth set into motion by such a change had to take place within the social framework provided by that order. Nothing in any way similar to what happened in the United States took place in Brazil. The country as a whole remained under the same slavocratic and seigneurial social order. Local variations arose to differing degrees of development, which permitted the economic, social, and political realization of this order (for example, São Paulo was a typical area of underdevelopment compared with Rio de Janeiro, Bahia, or Pernambuco). The economic sector emerging in some cities (of which Rio de Janeiro would be the prototype) was "new" as regards the nature of its institutional patterns and the tendencies regulating the organization and functioning of the market, which absorbed not only "internal" (local and regional) trade, but also and principally exports and imports with a large part of their financial offshoots (credit to producers, commodity trading, speculation in exportable primary products, and gradually, mortgages on real property and the various business transactions that fueled urban commerce and the growth of the urban commercial complex). Nonetheless, one thing bears mentioning: the urban commercial economy was practically a new sector. There are strands of continuity between the development of the cities *before* and *after* independence, above all on the economic plane. But the colony had been unable to forge even the material basis of such a process. The problem with the colonial market was not only one of size: it was also one of structure and function, even considering the cities that had really flourished in the colony. This was a market organized economically, technically, and institutionally to prevent any internal or outward-oriented growth that was not compatible with the dimensions and the future of a colonial economy. In this regard, the Portuguese were late in attempting a policy of reform, and then it was not with the purpose of making the colonial economy more flexible. The first efforts in the direction of modernization not explicitly tailored to specifically colonial patterns of internal growth were those connected with the transfer of the Court and the opening of the ports.* All this helps to show how narrowly the organization and dynamics of the internal market were conceived (with exceptions that only confirm the rule), with small interest devoted either to its urban pole or to the creative functions of commerce in an emergent capitalist economy. The "generation of independence" (and those that followed) set itself the task of economic progress in clearly seigneurial terms, with precedence given to the "interests of export agriculture" as "the source of the nation's wealth."[8] Thus the economic growth set off by the unfolding internal capitalist market—which finally was to eclipse and overcome the old colonial market—was not fueled by economic interests that were strong enough to enable the internal market to attain a position of preeminence in overall economic policy. The most advanced modernizing efforts stopped short at the frontiers of the conglomerated economic system of compromise, which invested the slavocratic and seigneural social order with privileges and reaffirmed the primacy of "archaic" economic forms in determining the dynamic equilibrium of the economic system as a whole. The slavocratic and seigneurial social order thus failed in essential respects: (1) it did not adapt the incipient tendencies toward formation of a capitalist market economy to the requirements of national economic integration and autonomous economic development on capitalist foundations; (2) it did not adapt these tendencies in such a way as to facilitate and accelerate the transition from the old market, inherited from the colonial period, to the new modern capitalist market; (3) it inhibited or neutralized tendencies toward the universalization of wage labor and the free play of strictly capitalist market relations. Indeed, in some areas it deliberately arrested the dissolution of the colonial market, which became a focus for the concentration of economic, social, and political change, limited mainly to export agricultural

---

*This occurred in 1808. The Portuguese king had fled Lisbon with the approach of Napoleon's armies.—Ed.

business and located mainly in the economically more robust cities.

However paradoxical it may seem then, the lack of flexibility of the slavocratic and seigneurial order immersed the generation of the period of independence and the generations that followed in the building of the foundations for dependent capitalism and the dead end that this represented for Brazil. The shift from a colonial pattern of economic growth to a pattern of capitalist development did not take place. Rather there was a linear succession from colonial growth to neocolonial growth and from these (quite rapidly) to the capitalist pattern of dependent economic growth and underdevelopment (a process similar to what took place in various countries in Europe, such as Spain and Portugal, and which was to be the pattern for all of Latin America). As it appears, things could not have transpired otherwise in Brazil; indeed, the gains achieved by the transition from the colony to an economically, socially, and politically dependent capitalism were considerable. Nonetheless, to use history as a device to explain the limitations on human actions is not a good method, since, after all, it is men who make history, and they do so socially. The fact that a country succumbs to a certain historical fate without desiring it is in itself a fact of real interpretive importance. It figures as an objective indication of the social aspirations and social will that motivate men as historical actors in their decisions and omissions, for the good or ill of the national society as a whole (in the particular moment as well as for the future). In the case in question, the capitalist world was clearly not the historical universe of the dominant social ranks; for this reason their elites did not face up to the present, nor did they foresee the future in this sense, i.e., capitalism as an aspiration and a style of life. They were totally immersed in an arduous defense of the very antithesis to the "bourgeois spirit" and "capitalist rationality." They struggled diligently to ensure the continued existence of slavery and seigneurial rule rather than its destruction and expeditious supersession. The forces that were to build up the capitalist economy and its competitive social order had therefore but this soil out of which to grow, on their own and against the mainstream, diffidently, destructively, and disorientedly, as if the true struggle for decolonization had not begun with political emancipation, but almost a century later.

Commerce and the organization of labor are the two levels of economic life in which this statement can be verified and proved empirically. Thus it is fitting to devote the final section of this analysis to these two aspects, which furthermore are especially apt for showing how the lack of flexibility related negatively to competition as a dynamic factor in motivating human actions and in regulating social relations.

In the capital and in some of the large cities, the shake-out of commerce to make way for the capitalist order began before political emancipation, thanks to the impact that the transference of the metropolitan government had on the dimensions and functioning of the internal market. Nevertheless, it was the dynamics of the world market, operating through the commercial and financial transactions of the export and import trade, and the establishment of a national state (as regards the juridical regulation of economic activities, legal and political constraints, and the government's political manipulation of market factors) which elevated this shake-out to the status of a normalizing factor in commercial relationships (monetarized or assessed in money terms, in credit transactions). Predominant commercial practices, however, continued to be regulated by traditional conventions, by economic guideposts that were of colonial origin and typical of a colonial conception of trade, as well as by usages specific to a society of estates. As a consequence, commerce had two distinct focal points, each with its own economic logic. In the export and import trade —"high commerce" as it was called, tied to the consumer patterns and style of life of the ruling ranks and geared to supplying the large plantations and to the wholesale trade—a typical capitalist orientation gradually took shape and grew in vigor (by dint of which transactions assumed *de facto* the characteristics of *business*). In "ordinary commerce," ranging from retail sales and small-scale handcraft trading to shipping and cargo services and street-peddling, a noncapitalist orientation tended to be perpetuated and even reinforced. Within it were gradations displaying the exploitative commerce typical of primitive accumulation of capital, as well as commercial transactions with all the formal and substantive characteristics of capitalism in the narrow sense. The "market mechanisms" of high commerce operated in a market that maintained its colonial connections and followed the logic of privilege of a seigneurial and monarchical economy, liberally applying exploitative principles that transformed costs and operating conditions into an element of risk and a factor of profit. On the other hand, in ordinary commerce, "market mechanisms" operated only tangentially insofar as they affected, directly or indirectly, the *position* of supply or of price estimates, whether arbitrary or "official." Nothing was able to impede their fluctuations, which were relatively irregular, or prohibit their more or less extortionate character. Despite the "political pressure" of the seigneurial sector to "keep a lid on high prices," the interests of the dominant ranks blended in various ways with such commercial practices and, together with labor contracts, they would be directly incorporated by many plantations in areas undergoing expansion.

These were the "material" aspects that shaped a market in transition from the colonial to the national eras. There was a considerable progress as compared with the chaos of the colonial market with its monopolies, privileges, prohibitions, and uncertainties. With political emancipation two regulatory and remedial influences came into play. First, there were the indirect or reactive social controls of the dominant ranks, who were no longer thwarted by metropolitan regulations. Internal means developed for exerting pressure on the "market," some of them institutionalized, others spontaneous and informal. Although such means were not (nor could they have been) fully effective from the economic standpoint, they exercised enormous influence in gradually eliminating vestiges from the past as well as in ensuring the progressive spread of certain minimal conditions for the normalization and growth of the internal market (as regards prices, product quality, the continuity and range of supply, etc.).[9] Second, as a result of the reorganization of the internal flow of profits, the buying power of the dominant ranks began to count in a purely economic sense (sometimes even following capitalist linkages, as occurred in the produce market and in the demand of the agricultural sector for foodstuffs). Moreover, the dismantling of colonial barriers gave a major boost to a kind of "low commerce," principally among the mass of the population. Little by little, especially in the large cities, the consumer capacity of this sector would also have a purely economic impact. On the whole, however, the structure of the economic system and the organization of society, both based on slave labor, worked against the constructive effects of these forces. It became practically impossible to universalize and institutionalize modern market mechanisms with slave labor and a segmentary free labor market existing side by side. A person who does not learn how to assess the market value of his labor will also not know how to measure his needs in market terms. Consequently, the institutional modernization of commerce, which was especially intense in the import and export business and in "high commerce," and the tendencies working to eliminate archaic economic practices fell as a matter of fact into a tremendous historical vacuum. Man, the central figure in the drama, did not step fully onto the market and refused to open the floodgates that would transform him in time into the very linchpin of economic life.

In this context, those branches of commercial activity that comprised the specifically or predominantly capitalist central core of the internal market imparted to it features peculiar to itself, and deformed it considerably (not to say irremediably). Privileged economically, socially, and politically, they rapidly if imperceptibly absorbed the values of the slavocratic and seigneurial social order. As a result, the austere businessman of the nascent prosperous urban "high commerce" adopted the same code of honor and aspired to the same ideals, and if he did not supersede, in any event strove to match the style of life of the rural aristocracy, confusing, against the backdrop of social change, the two psychologically different worlds of the *"Casa Grande"* and the *"Sobrado."* His supreme goal gradually shifted to acquiring seigneurial status through the acquisition of noble rank or some sign of favor to crown his "economic success," sublimating and dignifying it with the prestige and values of a caste and estate society. Such an outcome was almost inevitable, since the conditioning resulting from economic socialization in the narrow sense was marginal to the slavocratic and seigneurial social order, and lacked the vitality and autonomy to overcome the more general and profound conditioning deriving from the community of interests, values, and style of life of the ruling estates. Those who were most visibly and viscerally *bourgeois* were not segregated into a separate estate; they were accepted— with reserve at first but later openly—into "high society," where "nobility" and "fortune" were merged into one. Nor could it have been otherwise, since the very structure of the social order merged together into the same civil society all those who belonged to the middling and upper ranks. Thus the socialization resulting from a

---

*These were names applied to the residences of the plantation owner and the wealthy urban merchant. Cf. Gilberto Freyre, *Masters and the Slaves*, 2d ed., rev. (New York, 1966), in the Portuguese original *Casa Grande e Senzala* [Great House and Slave Quarters] ; and *The Mansions and the Shanties* (New York, 1963), in the Portuguese original *Sobrados e Mucambos.* —Ed.

community of interests and values spread from the seigneurial and truly hegemonic estate to the others, creating a solidarity among them and making them all "dominant."

But this was of little practical importance during the wave of modernization imposed by the internal development of a capitalist market. In this context commerce was the dynamic sector which brought with it the constitution of a "modern" infrastructure. Down to the end of the century this would be the truly innovative and advanced sector of the economy and the nucleus *par excellence* around which the entire new economic order would be built. From it derived the impetus, a considerable portion of the resources, and even the initiative for various undertakings, some quite bold, some less so, in industry, the service sector, communications and transport. Even so, the limiting effects mentioned were soon felt. Generally, socialization to the interests, values, and lifestyle of a community of estates attuned the driving forces of the commercial sector to the power (social and economic, and politically oriented as well as specifically political power) orientations of the agrarian aristocracy. The aristocracy held the reins over the "general course of the country" and knew how to promote the identification of the commercial sector with the defense of the existing order, containing or responding to the strongest aspirations of the commercial sector and dispelling any risk of its undertaking a "revolution within the order."

These aspects of the social destiny of the new economic interests, which carried such weight within the civil society, are truly important for sociological analysis. They enable us to observe better how and why an economic process that began as a torrent and evolved impetuously throughout the entire period of its consolidation, was deflected profoundly and irreversibly by the sociohistorical conditions within which it transpired. It stimulated economic growth of a new and innovative type; however, in itself this growth was not of sufficient size and intensity to destroy or at least transform radically the slavocratic and seigneurial social order. On the contrary, it was obliged to adapt to the structures of that order, and to the pace of its functioning and growth, until in the end it was literally molded and sapped of its own strength by it. As would happen later with the industrial sector, the commercial sector, because of its socioeconomic impotence—but also because it lacked a political impetus of its own—allowed the "general interests" (which were the "interests of the Country and of agriculture") to nullify the "interests of commerce" or permit them systematically to wither.

The principal effects of the situation just portrayed showed up on three different levels. First, the key link in the process of capitalist modernization, and the only one truly assimilated, either partially or completely (depending on what aspects of it are considered) to the needs and functions of a capitalist market, merely extended the dynamics of urban development into the heart of the existing order (its estate structure). Thus, investiture with the privileges of the estates could take place (above and beyond the specific limits set by economic processes). But it inevitably impaired and ultimately lost its capacity to act in a free and revolutionary way out of purely economic considerations, depriving the urban commercial economy of spokesmen capable of acting in the name of "rebellion within the established order." Second, by aligning its interests, its values, and its power structures with the ultimate position of the agrarian aristocracy, the most dynamic sector of the economy found itself forced to close its eyes to its dependent relation with the external market and to accept whatever came its way in the social process of commercialization of this relationship. Worst of all, owing to its strategic position in the process of institutional modernization and internal growth of capitalism, this sector served as a link to external influences and ties of dependency, without acquiring any critical awareness of the long-term baleful consequences of arrangements that at first glance or in the short run may have appeared the "best." Little by little, "private enterprise" and an association of dependence with foreign firms, interests, and capital, became the one and only reality by which this sector steered its economic and political action over the short and long term, adapting itself to the express expectations or preferences of the parent firms and submitting with no major resistance to an indirect yet clearly visible external domination.

Third, in organizing itself as an economic group, the commercial sector naturally relied on the estates for the source of its social and political power and on external sources for its economic power. The blending of the two did not detract from the vitality of the new economic sector, which continued to grow, at least in those periods when the external conditioning and driving forces contributed positively to institutional modernization and differentiation of the internal economy. But as soon as external influences ceased to stimulate and the internal market began to exert pressure on slave labor and slave-based production, the artificial and harmful nature of this accommodation of power became apparent. It was "high commerce," organized around the export and import business, which came up with the most efficient and most destructive ways to obstruct and undermine both the expansion of small-scale commerce, which concentrated on mass consumer goods, and the differentiation of production (especially in those branches that might diminish or threaten the position of imported goods). Only after the disintegration of the slavocratic and seigneurial order had reached clear and unmistakable proportions was this basic orientation relaxed and modified until a measure of compatibility was reached between the interests of "high commerce" and the internal drift of capitalist development. Despite the role that the great pioneers of the merchant trade played in this turnabout, it was not a "victory" of which the sector could boast collectively. These personages, and the conditions under which they achieved capitalist success, demonstrated graphically that the "leap forward" was the product of daring ruptures (and not, as is frequently claimed, of a gradual evolution of the entire sector toward a radical and consistent economic rationalism).

From what has just been described, the interdependence between the interests of the rural aristocracy and the interests of the nascent "urban bourgeoisie" was not a by-product of the free play of economic processes. A reciprocity between economic interests did exist, but it was not the material foundation upon which the political community was based; that came from a strong process of conditioning of the slavocratic and seigneurial order, which caused the social strata linked to "high commerce" to identify with the existing power structures. Therefore, there did not emerge a full-fledged "bourgeoisie," conscious of its historical mission and able to assert itself as the bearer of a specifically revolutionary consciousness. Reality shows us a contrary picture, for on the plane on which the actions of these social strata were profoundly and irrepressibly innovative, they set their sights on an evolution *with* and not *against* the agrarian aristocracy (thereby depriving the impetus of the "revolution within the system" of any political effectiveness). The innovations introduced were confined to adapting the national economy to economic functions that might be dynamized by the growth of the internal market. The incorporation of large-scale plantation agriculture into capitalism did not take place at the level of relations of production, but in terms of the econom-

ic roles objectified (or potentially objectifiable) in market relations; the seigneurial elites, seeing that these innovations concurred
with the interests of the rural aristocracy, began to support them.
Commerce, on the other hand, functioned largely as an economic
"sector" or "group," and to that extent it merely expressed the interests of "high commerce" (which had means and power to organize itself with a view toward economic and political ends). In
those areas where profound discontent prevailed, embracing all the
various sectors of "petty" and "low" commerce, conditions did
not exist for channeling economic or political discontent into collective and national action. Indeed, the situation in these areas was
one of explosive unrest, produced by the extreme pressures on
those sectors of commerce that were unable to attain to privileged
status on account of the nature of their business or the social level
of their clientele or of the merchants themselves. The pressure on
"petty" and "low" commerce was not relieved (nor could it have
been) simply through extinction of colonial status. There were
other factors contributing to this pressure, factors related to slave
labor, the slave system of production, the lack of differentiation
and vitality in the "national" economy, foreign sources of supply,
the supremacy of the "great merchants" and "wholesalers," the
weakness and cost of credit, dependence on the tolerance or protection of local notables, the relative marginality of the "small
businessman," etc.

Free commerce inevitably interfered with the slave-master
relationship in both city and countryside. Some of the goods and
the earnings gained by urban slaves ended up in the cash registers
of small shops and bars (not in the master's pocket); and the products received in exchange were consumed on the spot or disappeared in the commercial cycle without a trace. Repression in the
countryside was more necessary (when theft and fencing put in
their appearance) and even achieved a degree of effectiveness,
since it was easier to subject the merchant to some kind of control
or intimidation. In the urban milieu it was more difficult, and in
the large city almost impossible. Foreign sources of supply almost
suffocated commerce, drastically reducing the regular and smooth
flow of trade. The control over the trade was concentrated by a
few foreign firms and their representatives or national associates.
Moreover, the most rewarding and lucrative trade was with clientele possessing relatively higher incomes and purchasing power,
who could not be easily exploited by small businessmen. Nonethe-

less, it seems that the principal source of frustration and rebellion lay in the social marginality of the small businessmen, in some cases even of those who could be called *middle-sized businessmen* (depending on the area of commercial activity). The lowered social position did not derive from the nature of the economic activity in itself (since it did not affect persons involved in "high commerce"), but from the marginal social position of the actors, who were not classified in any of the social levels of the middling ranks.

Both separately and conjointly these factors gave rise to severe tensions and social frustrations. Nonetheless, these merchants accommodated to the situation, preferring to step up their personal efforts to "overcome barriers" and seeking the solutions to their problems in social mobility and the attainment of social worth within the estate structure. For this reason, the bulk of these economic actors were manipulated in struggles among the parties and in matters of political concern to "high commerce" and even to the rural aristocracy, who demanded support in popular demonstrations. Not even the campaign of the Republican Party during the Empire was able to galvanize this form of resentment and discontent. It was the abolitionist campaign which brought them together around a negation of the established order, in a condemnation of slavery and seigneurial domination. In sum, "bourgeois protest," as a revolutionary economic, social, and political statement, did not emerge historically from collective demonstrations condemning the slavocratic and seigneurial social order or exalting an alternative social order, for a very simple reason: the human agent best incarnating the *bourgeois condition* did not conspire against that social order. He identified with it materially and politically and would only abandon it when it proved to have become irremediably unviable as a result of profound social and economic changes, and not because of superficial unrest which, in the given case, far from steering history was an epiphenomenon of those changes.

Nonetheless, this human actor is of serious concern to sociological analysis. He is, after all, at the root of the formation of the Brazilian model of "competition." It would be unfair to underestimate the creative effort—in the purely economic sense—of the human actor involved in the "high commerce" of the export and import trade. But it would also be naive to attempt to understand him as if he had been at the command of economic processes in a self-sustained, self-sufficient, and hegemonic capitalist development. He was the finished product of the "piracy" and the extortionate character of the neocolonial trade that English *indirect rule* spread throughout the world. There was an economic substrate in the "terms of the contract"; however, trade did not consist of a strictly economic operation taking place within a modern, strictly capitalist market. What counted in neocolonial commerce was essentially the capacity to dictate or determine the conditions of trade. Like the agrarian sector, the "mercantile sector" would define its understanding of "private enterprise" and the nature of "competition" in estate-bound terms: as a privilege, or as the ability to influence or set the conditions within which economic relations and processes would have to be adapted to the situation as defined by the interests of the economic actor. From this viewpoint, the latter did not fulfill his economic destiny in and through the market, but above and beyond it, through the manipulation of power structures susceptible of regulating, directly or indirectly, fluctuations in costs, prices, and profit. This purely instrumental notion of "private initiative" and "competition" perverted economic action, investing it with privilege and power independent of "market forces" (and, depending on the circumstances, even against them). Nonetheless, this notion did not just promote the political integration of the mercantile sector, but persisted throughout the entire subsequent development of the capitalist market in Brazil.

In a number of respects, this was the chief fruit bequeathed by the slavocratic and seigneurial social order to the formation of the "bourgeois spirit" in Brazilian society. "Private enterprise" and "competition," rightly understood within this sociohistorical context, could be used both to the advantage and to the detriment of economic development. As a rule they were and have continued to be extremely harmful because they demand and reinforce interference with the "normal course" of economic processes and because they thereby create an uncontrollably speculative climate in mercantile relationships. From the standpoint of the economic actor, they were and continue to be useful since they normally guarantee special conditions of return and security in commercial transactions in dependent economies. As long as the slavocratic and seigneurial social order stayed in dynamic equilibrium, thereby ensuring its own stability and continued existence, this predatory model of "private enterprise" and "competition" exerted constructive influences (one factor in which was economic and institutional changes that strengthened and differentiated that social order or served as a basis for processes of "revolution within the system," necessary for political emancipation). This model was at the root of the economic, social, and political philosophy that harmonized the interests of the agrarian and mercantile sectors through a hybrid economic system of accommodation. When the social order itself entered into crisis, failing to ensure through its power structures the normal and advantageous functioning of this model, it abruptly revealed its disintegrating potential. It acted neither as a "social yeast" requiring a long historical ferment, nor as a "purely revolutionary element" bearing with it a new utopia. Rather, it was a factor atomizing the slavocratic and seigneurial social order, because it caused that order to lose the "confidence" of the mercantile sector as soon as the social and political sources of its economic efficacity disappeared.

The colonial system of production left its most profound and lasting marks on labor. In a social order exclusively and specifically of estates, such as took root and evolved on the Iberian peninsula (in this respect the differences between Portugal and Spain are unimportant), artisan labor and the kind of commerce it engendered possessed their own area of social differentiation and growth. "Physical labor" inevitably bore a stigma that was almost as degrading as the stigma of blood, both of which were transferred to the colonial world. "Physical labor," nevertheless, was one of the material foundations for the slow elaboration and expansion of the "town economy." In the colony, however, the superimposition of slavery on the estate system brought about an extreme degradation of "physical labor" and imposed completely new standards for supplementing slave labor with the labor of "free" or "semi-servile" men: freedmen and dependent *homens livres*, both excluded from the estate order; artisans, "trusted associates," and poor relatives belonging to the dominant race and hence part of the order of estates. The numbers reflecting this situation established an inescapable reality: the notion of "work" applied to "physical" jobs, work under the direction and for the benefit of others, and in one way or other presupposed the loss of social dignity and freedom. To escape from this onus, artisans arriving from Europe would try to avoid practical work (which was relatively easy given the abundance of land and the precarious nature of coercive controls) or practiced their trades as if they were ornamental journeymen or masters, leaving to the slave everything they regarded as physical, such as the loading of materials and supplies and the carrying out of all the simpler tasks. In addition, the journeymen and masters worked at a pace that enabled them to control demand, so that placing an order with them became an extremely problematic and vexatious social exchange. The mercantilization of labor was not obstructed by slavery alone. It also clashed with the functional limitations of the colonial market, which did not classify persons and social groups in a system of estates and castes, and with the dictates of custom whereby the labor of men of "good standing" was not a commodity. Thus, mercantilization was not only incipient and segmentary, it was also occasional or marginal, and as such resisted transformation into a normal, impersonal, and desirable relationship. It was the slave who was defined automatically as a commodity by the market, and not the slave's labor. With regard to the slave, there was no question of selling or purchasing labor since it was the *slave* who was purchased or rented, and his owner disposed of the slave, including his abilities, aptitudes, and labor power, as he wished.

The persistence of slavery in both the countryside and the town was responsible for this entire colonial complex of labor being perpetuated throughout the nineteenth century, hindering the formation, differentiation, and expansion of a genuine labor market alongside the slave market and facilitating the ultra-exploitation of freedmen and the semi-servile and free persons who lived from their labor power. This impelled a dichotomous economic evolution: the urban commercial economy, in which free labor as a commodity first emerged and expanded, grew parallel with the exclusion of the slave, yet it was the slave who in the final analysis produced the economic surplus that made possible and stimulated that growth. Thus, the immediate achievements of modernization and the dose of decolonization inherent in national emancipation did not free the slave nor liberate the economy from slave labor. On the contrary, neocolonial modernization and controlled decolonization would be nourished by the wholesale perpetuation of the colonial system of production on which would come to depend the viability of national emancipation, the continued existence and expansion of the slavocratic and seigneurial social order after independence, the emergence of the capitalist market in the urban commercial sector, etc. Although slavery was the foundation of both the capitalist development of the hegemonic countries that controlled the tropical market and of the incipient internal capitalist development (limited, during the transitional turn of the nineteenth century, to the "new" or urban commercial sector of the economy), changes in the relationship between slavery and capitalism neither affected the slave nor altered the ties of slave labor to the system of production since both—slave labor and the system of production—continued to be typically colonial. Consequently, slave labor continued, closely tied to heavy manual labor, supporting occupations, or domestic services, etc., where the difference between the rural and urban economies was nil or almost nil. The various attempts to carry slave labor into other economic domains and frontiers—principally by dint of differentiation of the system of production and manufacturing—where the slave could appear to be an equivalent to free labor and an agent of the emergent new economic order, failed dramatically over and over again. This was not only because the slave was not trained for his new tasks, but also, and especially, because as long as the colonial pattern of production was maintained neither the effectiveness nor productivity of slave labor could be broadened and differentiated. The problem, then, was organizational, and the "victims of the colonial system of production" were inevitably the slave and the freedman, both condemned from the very beginning to suffer the most negative and destructive consequences of the concomitant development of the old economic sector, linked to colonial production, persisting *en bloc* and growing with the reorganization of the export trade, and the new sector, linked to the emergence and expansion of the urban commercial centers.

But once the brief neocolonial phase was past and the crisis caused by the imperative emancipationist measures was at its peak, the central economic roles shifted from slave to free labor. Despite its weakness, free labor by the middle of the nineteenth century was already becoming the cornerstone of the expanding urban economic system, which was spreading into the countryside. Slave labor, historically essential for the viability of agrarian production and the estate order, however, also influenced and determined inexorable tendencies. Free labor did not emerge in a market that divides and opposes, but at the same time rewards and upgrades. It emerged as the expression of conventions and patterns regnant in the stifling Brazilian seigneurial and slavocratic social order. Instead of stimulating competition and conflict, it came into the world exhausted, entrenching itself structurally and dynamically in a climate of command, paternalism, and conformity imposed by the existing society, as if free labor were merely a category of slave labor. The break that was to take place in the last quarter of the nineteenth century was more "mechanical" and "static" than societal, historical, and political; a mere outcome of the existing incompatibilities between slave labor and free labor, the colonial market and the capitalist market, and colonial production and capitalist production. The freed man and the dependent *homem livre* were no real alternatives in areas of intense and rapid economic growth as far as the restructuring of the system of labor within both commercial urban economy and the rural economy was concerned. As took place with capitalist development of the internal market, the spread of free labor would begin as a process furthering the incorporation into the world market through foreign immigration and government-sponsored settlement colonies. Thus the flood began, which was also to absorb gradually, albeit irregularly and unsystematically, the *homens livres* and semi-servile workers of the domestic population (freedmen and the slaves emancipated *en masse* at Abolition were also part of the flood, but under special conditions that cannot be dealt with here).

What was important about this break was not labor in itself, but demographic composition and equilibrium. The pattern changed rapidly, in areas of economic growth. In less than three quarters of a century, from the termination of the slave traffic [1850] (as the development of the population of São Paulo testifies),[10] the new demographic pattern required by an economic system based on free labor emerged and spread. This process provided the material substrate for the "revolution within the system" and for the abolitionist and Republican struggles against the *ancien régime*. As demographic composition and equilibrium changed, propensities to identify or clash with the slavocratic and seigneurial social order also changed. What the capitalist labor market did not create by its own emergence, it would supply by the socioeconomic polarizations of the various segments of the entire population. It may be said that the slavocratic and seigneurial social order lost almost all at once the material bases for its demographic and economic existence, and this did not take place suddenly only because of the slowness with which the critical breaking point was reached. The labor shortage on the plantations and in the cities in the areas experiencing economic growth facilitated the transition, relieved it of any catastrophic ingredient, and reoriented the demographic and economic patterns of bourgeois society. The situation

of the freedman in this general process was better than that of the
ex-slaves; however, as the slaves disappeared, his role as an alternative also diminished. The ex-slave felt the destructive impact of the
transition, since he had to face the competition of immigrants and
of the free or semi-servile national workers, the discriminating
treatment of the employers, and self-assessments that predisposed
him to resist wage labor, as if this were merely a continuation of
the status of slave. But he was not alone in these critical moments.
Divers sectors of the population did not fully understand the nature of free labor and wage labor, as if it were difficult or impossible to separate labor as a commodity from the worker's person.
This structural situation was to complicate the entire historical
process, long delaying the emergence of a working class consciousness, and weakening the legitimate use of competition and conflict
in typically contractual relations, which Brazilians tended to view
as traditional relations of loyalty or typically patrimonial relations.
In turn, the master who became a boss (and frequently the arche-
typal boss of the urban centers) reacted correspondingly (often
enough, this was not a new reaction, since in city and countryside
alike it was not uncommon to use slave labor and free labor side
by side). For him too, the worker sold his person in some sense
along with his labor, creating ties and obligations that went beyond market relations, perpetuating traditionalism and patrimonialism by the secularization of culture. Some time and many re-
educative conflicts were necessary for the labor contract and free
labor to consolidate their positions, relatively slowly and with considerable irregularity, at this pole of "wage relations."[11] The immigrant here and there established himself more impellingly, being
the kind of labor power favored by the course of history, and did
much to spread new forms of working-class behavior. However, before the peak of the crisis and the irreversible point of transition
was reached, he too found himself, as worker, deprived of social,
economic, and political power. Neither he nor workers in general
had the means to bring the weight of their interests or their values
and aspirations to bear on the demographic and economic process
just described. The transformation of labor into a commodity and
its elaboration as a constructive and relatively autonomous social
factor were not concomitant processes. Indeed, "free labor" appeared first as a commodity, as a reality on the capitalist market
and in the emerging system of capitalist production that extended
from city to countryside. Only afterward, with the final crisis over

and the slavocratic and seigneurial social order finally departed from the scene, did "free labor" become a constructive social factor, adapting itself to the social and political functions it had to assume in the competitive social order. Thus, under the First Republic,* labor completed the full circle of its transformation into a pure commodity. For this to be achieved a person who sold his labor had to be able to count at least on some economic, social, and political conditions that would enable him to define and insist on his side of the wage bargain and the relationship between boss and laborer.

The foregoing discussion underscores a number of points that are already well known. The wage privileges not the worker, but the person appropriating labor and its products. The difference between the old slavocratic and seigneurial social order and the modern competitive social order is that in the former, appropriation had no external regulators of real effectiveness, while in the latter, the market, living standards and wage levels, competition and conflict (initially polarized only by the trade-union movement), working-class consciousness and class solidarity (which emerge gradually), the militant and nonconformist political participation of the poor and wage laborers, and so forth, little by little transformed "national integration" into a democratic and revolutionary process which at least broke down archaic social barriers and introduced "social class leveling mechanisms." This process had roots in national emancipation and in the correlative tendencies of modernization controlled from without, in the development of an internal capitalist market, and in the growth of urban commerce. Nonetheless, since the initial decolonization was minimal, owing to the preservation of slavery, colonial production, and the slavocratic and seigneurial social order, first seigneurial domination and then its transformation, oligarchic domination, blocked the formation of classes and mechanisms of class solidarity, economically, socially, and politically, imposing instead conservative control and autocratic power by the elites of the dominant classes as the conducting wire of history. The historical gamut of the transition of colonial society into imperial society was once more repeated. Those who had wealth and political power were able to invest with privilege their interests and class positions, accelerating this social for-

---

*The designation of the Republican governments under the Constitution of 1891, lasting until 1930.—Ed.

mation at the top and preventing as far as possible its consolidation on the basis of the competitive social order. As a result, these persons placed themselves in a position that enabled them to maintain privileges which normally could not have subsisted (i.e., if the poor and the wage laborers had had analogous opportunities to accelerate the development and consolidation of the class system). It also enabled them to transform the divers requirements of the competitive social order into closed privileges, beginning with the monopolization of wealth and power, making oligarchic rule under the republic a "democracy among equals," i.e., a rigid class dictatorship. What interests us here is that the sources of the negative socialization of labor, both slave and free, could only be combatted tardily, during the historical processes of specific political struggle against seigneurial domination, and later against its successor, oligarchic rule.

In reality, however, the negative socialization of slave labor was never arrested, and the negative socialization of free labor became a social issue only quite recently under the pressure of the trade-union movement and the political nonconformity of the working class. This means that, during the formation and expansion of the competitive social order, free labor was subjected to a process of long-term corruption which began by denying it the conditions of solidarity as an estate (under the *ancien régime*) and ended by denying it the conditions of solidarity as a class (under the class regime and the Republic). This deprived and still deprives free labor of the structural and dynamic foundations necessary for its elaboration into a constructive social factor, capable of fueling and giving direction to change from below in the competitive social order. In the past, the dominant estates thought of the workers only in terms of final costs (of production or of services) and regarded them socially as disqualified from valid dialogue.[12] This universe, which maintained itself for a long time despite various reform and revolutionary movements among the poor population and the working class, was unable to impart economic, social, legal, or political efficacy to the labor contract, to free competition, or to a controlled or legitimate conflict. Free labor (like slave labor) evolved in the most cynical and brutal manner, as a pure instrument of economic exploitation and of the most intensive capital accumulation possible. The human element or human dimension of labor, like "social peace," are rhetorical devices of explicit bourgeois mystification, and when they have to go further, traditionalist paternalism and authoritarianism give way to police repression and politico-military dissuasion.[13]

Translated by Michel Vale

NOTES

1. A terrain, furthermore, in which the question was posed by the rural aristocracy in formal terms of national sovereignty.

2. Clearly the pattern described was applied to the nature and the functions of competition with reference to other economic actors (whatever the basis of its mercantile operations, i.e., whether commercial or manufacture), since all protected themselves in one way or other through privileges of rank. What happened in the primary sector was repeated in all the others.

3. This description, couched in quite summary terms, contains the unequivocal recommendation that this type of middling rank must not be confused with the middle sector of a class society and even less with a "middle class" or a "petite bourgeoisie" in process of formation. Actually, with the later transformations in Brazilian society, a broad segment of these ranks were gradually transformed into the emergent middle classes. However, in the situation under consideration here they appeared rather as a replication of the past (and not as a "force of the future") and contributed little in themselves to any further development.

4. Honorable status was a commonplace acquisition, variously attainable. Noble status was rarer and more difficult. Both could transcend wealth, and qualified those individuals moving upward to share in the style of life and privileges of the seigneurial rank (in the countryside and in the city).

5. This analysis completely bears out the bitter reflections of Nabuco on the underlying causes of the disintegration of Imperial society mentioned in the preceding chapter [of *A Revolução Burguesa no Brasil*] (cf. Joaquim Nabuco, *Minha Formação* [3rd ed.; São Paulo, 1947], pp. 178-79).

6. The different development of São Paulo does not vitiate this description. The plantation owners of the São Paulo West, São Paulo businessmen, and politicians of rural origin had their share of vacillation and resistance in moving ahead toward the rationalization of slave-based production and in the question of abolition. It was only when they no longer had anything to defend that they took the final steps, proving that the bourgeois condition predominated over the seigneurial element in them. As we have shown above, all of this was possible only because they were unable to identify themselves profoundly with the seigneurial style and patterns of existence. As a consequence, as soon as they first appeared on the historical scene, they set into motion the real transition from one regime to the other.

7. In regard to the first alternative, it was the idea of taking advantage of the opportunities of a "colonial economy" (which the Brazilian economy continued to be for a long time) to give an accelerated but directed boost to internal economic growth that would prevail. In the second, it was the ambition of linking political autonomy with independent capitalist growth that would have predominated (as took place in the United States during the period of independence).

8. It would be interesting to pursue the parallel with the United States. There the "generation of independence," with foresight and tremendous keenness of vision, preferred to lay the legal, political, and economic foundations of self-sustained and hegemonic capitalist development.

9. Clearly such achievements had their locus in the urban economy and spread only slowly and unsystematically into the small cities and villages.

10. See Florestan Fernandes, "O Negro em São Paulo," in J. V. Freitas Marcondes and O. Pimentel, *São Paulo, Espírito, Povo, Instituiçoes*.

11. As a typical example see the testimony of Davatz, in particular the interpretations of Sergio Buarque de Holanda in Tomas Davatz, *Memorias de um colono no Brasil* (2nd ed.; São Paulo, 1951).

12. This explains the extremely low wages the coffee plantation owners paid the immigrants—see Emilia Viotti da Costa, *Da Senzala à Colônia* (São Paulo, 1966); and the treatment of working-class protest as a police matter —see Everardo Dias, *Historia das Lutas Sociais no Brasil* (São Paulo, 1962).

13. The other two questions are not taken up.

THE AUTOCRATIC
BOURGEOIS MODEL
OF CAPITALIST
TRANSFORMATION

The relationship between bourgeois domination and capitalist transformation is highly variable. Contrary to what might be supposed on the basis of a Europocentric conception (which is valid in any event only for the classic cases of bourgeois revolution), there is no one basic democratic bourgeois model of capitalist transformation. Social scientists have demonstrated that capitalist transformation is not determined exclusively by the intrinsic requirements of capitalist development. On the contrary, these requirements (whether they be economic, sociocultural, or political) interact with various extracapitalist or precapitalist economic and noneconomic elements of the specific sociohistorical situation, and thus suffer obstructions, selections, and adaptations. Together, these delineate the concrete historical social terms under which capitalist transformation will take place; the concrete pattern of bourgeois domination, including the reconciliation of nonbourgeois and bourgeois class interests, as well as external class interests if relevant, and the absorption of economic, sociocultural, and political elements extrinsic to capitalist transformations; and the eventuality of bourgeois absorption of the central economic, sociocultural, and political requirements of capitalist transformation and, conversely, of the capitalist transformation accompanying those structural, functional, and historical polarizations of bourgeois domination that might be historically constructive and creative.

Until recently the only manifestations regarded as warranting

From *A Revolução Burguesa no Brasil: Ensaio de Interpretação* (Rio de Janeiro: Zahar Editores, 1976), pp. 289-366.

designation as bourgeois revolution were those that approximated in their typical features the "classic" cases in which there was a maximum of fluidity in the reciprocal relations between capitalist transformation and bourgeois domination. This was at the least a one-sided position that lost sight of the empirical, theoretical, and historical significance of "ordinary" cases in which bourgeois revolution appears linked to structural and dynamic changes impelled by the outward reach of mature capitalism, or of "atypical" cases in which the bourgeois revolution displays a sequence of events quite different from the way it developed in England, France, and the United States. Studies of Germany and Japan are to the point.

More important for this chapter, from a theoretical point of view, is the relationship between capitalist transformation and bourgeois domination in peripheral countries with dependent and underdeveloped capitalist economies. For a long time two erroneous assumptions limited the penetration and the explanatory force of sociological analyses of these cases. The first, quite common, assumption regards the "stages" of the bourgeois revolution— thought to be identical to those of the central and hegemonic capitalist societies. The prevailing idea was that dependence and underdevelopment were transitory stages destined to disappear by dint of the ineluctable, progressive autonomy of capitalist development. Accordingly, it would be legitimate to assume that the dependent and underdeveloped periphery would tend to repeat—once the anticolonial revolution had taken place and the initial stage of neo-colonial transition had been passed—the history of the central nations. It was not recognized that capitalist expansion of the dependent periphery was fated to be permanently remodeled by the dynamics of the central capitalist economies and the world capitalist market. Rosa Luxemburg made this quite clear in her general theory of capitalist accumulation.[1] Second, it was overlooked that autonomous capitalist development requires as a precondition a break with external domination (colonial, neocolonial, or imperialist).[2] As long as this domination persists, what takes place is *dependent* capitalist development, which, no matter what its tendencies, is incapable of fulfilling all the economic, sociocultural, and political functions of the corresponding stage of capitalism. Clearly capitalist growth occurs, accompanied by an accelerating accumulation of capital and institutional modernization, yet at the same time external capitalist expropriation and relative underdevelopment persist as ineluctable conditions and effects. Moreover, even if autonomous capitalist development should become "automatic," this would not in itself ensure a uniform path either of capitalist development or of the consolidation of bourgeois domination (as might be supposed from the frequent comparison of the United States with Japan).

The picture is therefore much more complex than what the initial assumptions allowed one to suppose. What is of particular theoretical importance for the present discussion is that the essential was overlooked. It was forgotten that what the dependent part of the periphery "absorbs" and consequently "repeats," as far as the "classic" cases are concerned, are essential structural and dynamic traits that characterize the existence of what Marx referred to as a mercantile economy, relative surplus value, etc., and the emergence of a differentiated competitive economy or an articulated monopolistic economy, etc. This guarantees some fundamental similarities, without which the dependent part of the periphery would not be *capitalist* and could not absorb the dynamics of growth or development of the central capitalist economies. These similarities—which do not account for the capitalist expropriation inherent in imperialist domination and therefore do not account for dependence or underdevelopment either—nevertheless overlay fundamental differences stemming from the process whereby capitalist development of the periphery becomes dependent, underdeveloped, and prey to imperialist domination, tying the central capitalist economies and the peripheral capitalist economies together into the same framework. In Marxist terms, it is these differences, not the similarities, which must be invoked to account for the essential and differential variations, i.e., that which is typical of capitalist transformation and bourgeois domination in dependent capitalism. Only in this way is it possible to show how and why the bourgeois revolution constitutes a historical reality unique to dependent and underdeveloped capitalist nations, without reifying or mystifying history. So the bourgeois revolution inevitably combines capitalist transformation and bourgeois domination. Nevertheless this combination takes place under specific economic and sociohistorical conditions which rule out the likelihood that "history repeats itself" or that the preconditions of the aforementioned democratic bourgeois model come about "automatically." On the contrary, what does occur, albeit with varying intensity, is a thoroughly *pragmatic* dissociation between capitalist development and democracy; or in positivist sociological terms, a thoroughly *rational* association between capitalist development and autocracy. Thus what is "good" for capitalist development comes into conflict with the democratic evolution of the social order, the conflict being manifested less in the values than in the concrete behavior of the possessing and bourgeois classes. The notion of "bourgeois democracy" undergoes a redefinition, dissimulated at the level of common usage but inexorably imposed as a practical reality, whereby this democracy is restricted to the possessing classes, who qualify economically, socially, and politically for the exercise of bourgeois domination.

The other wrong assumption concerns the essence of bourgeois domination in dependent and underdeveloped capitalist economies. The effects of the inhibition of the political elements of dependent capitalism or, alternatively, of the regressive differentiation of bourgeois power, were associated with imperialism, although they were not compatible with any form of bourgeois domination and much less with the kind of bourgeois domination specifically required by the dependent and underdeveloped capitalist nations. It was overlooked that the double appropriation of the economic surplus—by the national bourgeoisie and by the bourgeoisies of the hegemonic capitalist superpowers—placed a tremendous pressure on the dependent and underdeveloped capitalist development, causing an accentuated hypertrophy of the social and political factors of bourgeois domination. The extreme concentration of wealth, the drain of a major portion of the national economic surplus abroad, the consequent persistence of pre- or subcapitalist forms of labor, and the fundamental depression of the value of wage labor, all contrasting with the high level of aspirations and with compensatory pressures for a democratization of economic, sociocultural, and political participation, worked severally and jointly to produce consequences that overburdened and suffocated the specifically political functions of bourgeois domination, both self-defensive and purely repressive. Thus were, and are, created those social and political requirements of capitalist transformation and bourgeois domination that have no counterparts in the capitalist development of the central and hegemonic nations—including those in which fascism produced the same general autocratic bourgeois model. In this respect, dependent and underdeveloped capitalism is a savage and unruly form of capitalism whose viability is frequently decided in the political arena. Con-

trary to what has been supposed and still is supposed in many intellectual circles, it is not true that the bourgeoisies and the governments of the hegemonic capitalist nations have any interest in
interfering with the flow of political events by deliberately weakening the dependent bourgeoisies or by any other means. If they
did so, they would encourage the development of bourgeoisies
with nationalist revolutionary leanings, within private capitalism,
or set into motion a transition to state capitalism or socialism.
They would thus be working against their most immediate interests, which consist in the continued development of dependent
and underdeveloped capitalism.

It is essential to stress this fact since it facilitates the compre-
hension of what happened and what is happening in Brazil and
other countries in an analogous situation in Latin America. What
might have happened, and occasionally did happen, in the period
of neocolonial transition would not be repeated afterwards, especially since the consolidation of the internal market brought about
a transition to more complex forms of capitalist development in
competitive capitalism and later—in an even more accentuated
form—in monopoly capitalism. The very fact that the neocolonial
situation was superseded points to the emergence of a bourgeoisie
with national roots. The other two later transitions testify in turn
to modifications of capitalist transformation and bourgeois domination during dependent capitalism, making the potential evolution of bourgeois power a historical reality. Hence the "weakness"
of bourgeoisies subjugated to and identified with imperialist domination is only relative. The more profound the capitalist transformation, the more the central and hegemonic capitalist nations require trustworthy partners in the dependent and underdeveloped
periphery. This means a bourgeoisie with national roots, sufficiently strong to carry out all the political functions of self-defense and
repression required by bourgeois domination. This need is even
more acute when imperialism is total, as it is inherently under
monopoly capitalism. Ever since World War II, having begun the
struggle for survival against the socialist regimes, these nations
have had to depend on the national bourgeoisies of the dependent
and underdeveloped capitalist nations to preserve or consolidate
capitalism in the periphery. The national bourgeoisies of these nations consequently became authentic "internal frontiers" and
genuine "political vanguards" of the capitalist world—that is, of

imperialist domination by monopoly capitalism. It is an illusion to think that this would reduce the political needs of dependent capitalism.

Such a situation enhances the importance of the political element in dependent and underdeveloped capitalist development. Not just the future potential, but the very survival of capitalist transformation and bourgeois domination turns on a specifically political axis. If the national bourgeoisies of the periphery should fail in this political mission, there would be neither capitalism nor class rule nor bourgeois hegemony over the state. All this suggests that the bourgeois revolution at the periphery is *par excellence* an essentially political phenomenon, creating, consolidating, and preserving structures that are predominantly political and subject to the control of the bourgeoisie or controllable by it, whatever the situation. Accordingly, if one regards the bourgeois revolution at the periphery as a "frustrated revolution," as many authors do (probably taking their cues from Gramsci's interpretation of the bourgeois revolution in Italy), one must proceed with extreme caution (or at least with Gramscian objectivity and circumspection). This is not an era of *bourgeoisies conquérants*. The national bourgeoisies of the periphery and the bourgeoisies of the central and hegemonic capitalist nations both have interests and orientations tending in another direction. They want to maintain order, safeguard and strengthen capitalism, and keep bourgeois domination and bourgeois control of the national state from deteriorating. These reciprocal interests and orientations cause the politics of dependent capitalism to present two interdependent aspects. Further, it ensures that the "backward" bourgeois revolution at the periphery is strengthened by a dynamic specific to world capitalism and is carried, almost systematically and universally, to profoundly reactionary political actions that reveal the autocratic essence of bourgeois domination and its propensity to safeguard its own existence by accepting open and systematic forms of class dictatorship.

Here we arrive at a general point of prime theoretical importance. It is not merely that the "laggard" bourgeois revolutions in the dependent and underdeveloped periphery were affected by the structural changes that had taken place in the advanced capitalist world. Clearly, the transformations that occurred in the central and hegemonic capitalist economies directly and indirectly deprived the peripheral bourgeoisies of their historically defined economic, social, and political roles. They found themselves without any material basis for realizing these roles, as a consequence of the confluent and compound effects of the drain of the national economic surplus, and of incorporation economically, culturally, and politically by the hegemonic capitalist nations and by imperialist domination. That, in a nutshell, is why bourgeois revolution was so late in coming in the dependent and underdeveloped periphery of the capitalist world. But there was another side to the coin. Though the bourgeois revolution was belated, history, on the other hand, took a jump forward. The bourgeoisies, which have only now reached the high point of their possibilities, under such difficult conditions, found themselves supporting a transformation of the established order that had lost all of its revolutionary significance. This transformation is part of the "bourgeois revolution" because it is part of a process that extends over time and is reflected in the contradictions of classes confronting one another with antagonistic historical goals. Essentially these bourgeoisies aspire to a revolution that for other classes embodies a veritable counter-revolution. The majority is no longer blind to the fact, whether they accept bourgeois options or openly oppose them, identifying themselves instead with the expectations raised by revolutionary or reformist socialism.

Under such circumstances, antagonistic revolutions coexist. One such revolution comes from the past and is brought to fruition without any major long-term perspectives. The other stakes out its territory in the "building of the future in the present." Whether one's aims are descriptive or interpretative, the implications of this and the repercussions such a sequence of circumstances has on the concrete aspects of class relations cannot be disregarded. Contrary to the currently popular view, bourgeoisies in dependent and underdeveloped capitalism are not merely "comprador" bourgeoisies, such as were typical of colonial and neocolonial situations in the strict sense. They possess considerable economic, social, and political power that has a national base and is national in scope; they control the machinery of the national state; and they can count on external support in modernizing the forms of socialization, cooptation, oppression, and repression intrinsic to bourgeois domination. It is very difficult, therefore, to budge them politically through pressures and conflicts "within the order," and it is almost impossible to use the political space secured by the legal system to bring class contradictions, further aggravated by the circumstances mentioned above, to the bursting point. The "delay" of the bourgeois revolution in the dependent and under-developed part of the periphery thus acquires a special political import. The bourgeoisie at the periphery is struggling not only to consolidate its relative advantages and maintain its privileges, it is also struggling for its survival and the survival of capitalism. This introduces a political element into its class behavior that has not been typical of capitalism, especially during the periods of eco-nomic, sociocultural, and political maturation of bourgeois domi-nation in Europe and the United States. This variation, purely his-torical, is nonetheless key to an understanding of the growing gap between bourgeois ideology and utopia and the reality created by bourgeois domination. These bourgeoisies have no alternative, in a strictly political sense (that is, in a "rational," "intelligent," or "deliberate" sense), to final ruin and ossification. Bourgeois ideal-ism must be put aside, together with its commitments to any au-thentic reformism, radical liberalism, or consistent democratic bourgeois nationalism. Thus are exposed to history all of the irre-ducible and essential features of bourgeois domination that ex-plain its "virtues" and "defects" as well as its "historic achieve-ments": its inflexibility and its decision to use institutionalized violence in the defense of private material interests and private po-litical ends, and its temerity in identifying itself with autocratic forms of self-defense and self-assumed privilege. Thus "bourgeois nationalism" begins its last act, merging the parliamentary repub-lic with fascism.

We are surely witnessing bourgeois power in its most extreme, brutal, and revealing historical manifestation, made both possible and necessary by its state of political paroxysm; it is a power that imposes itself without disguise from above, using any means to prevail, setting itself up as its own source of legitimacy, and finally transforming the national and democratic state into a pure instru-ment of a preventive class dictatorship.

Whether we like it or not, this is the reality with which we are faced and with regard to which we can harbor no illusions. The most that may be said is that democracy and nationalist identifica-tions would have endured this bourgeois power *if* capitalist trans-formation and bourgeois domination had assumed (or could have assumed) at one and the same time other forms and other histor-ical rhythms.

The links between bourgeois domination and capitalist transformation underwent some relatively rapid change as competitive capitalism in Brazil was consolidated, developed, and spread, and in particular as the transition to monopoly capitalism became more intensive and rapid. The central element in this change was of course the emergence of industrialization as a basic economic, social, and cultural process that modified the organization, the dynamics, and the position of the urban economy within the Brazilian economic system. Seen from this perspective, urban and metropolitan hegemony appears as a by-product of the hegemony of the industrial-financial complex. Not only does this process alter the economic, sociocultural, and political dynamics of the major cities with metropolitan functions; it also brings about and later intensifies the concentration of material, human, and technical resources in these cities, giving rise to all the characteristic phenomena of metropolization and satellitization in dependent capitalism. What these phenomena demonstrate first and foremost is that the relations of the cities with the agrarian economy on the one hand and the urban commercial complex on the other, underwent a total change without causing any real disintegration in the dual articulation of the dependent capitalist economy [that is, uneven internal development and external imperialist domination].

The changes in the relationships between bourgeois domination and capitalist transformation, which may be viewed and described either structurally or dynamically, in the case of Brazil followed the historical rhythms characteristic of national dependent and underdeveloped economies. The changes were spread out over a long period of time, giving rise to a pattern of industrialization sensitive to the ups and downs of the business cycle, structural irregularities, and institutional inconsistencies, with only weak intrinsic tendencies toward differentiation, acceleration, and universalization of industrial growth. As a consequence, the historical impact of these changes showed up more glaringly at the surface (in morphological terms), e.g., in the concentration of human masses, wealth, and modern technologies in a few key metropolises. Indeed, only São Paulo was able to capitalize on these fundamental transformations; the basic change in scenario was reflected in a general sense more at the summit of the class system, since only those groups occupying strategic positions (central, intermediary, or intermediate) during the economic cycle of intensive industrialization experienced any real (and indeed disproportional) increase in their socioeconomic and political power.

This picture would appear to warrant our resuming the analytic and expository approach taken in the first part of this essay, whereby for purposes of sociological description we regarded the last three quarters of the century as a single inclusive whole. A point in favor of this approach is that it facilitates a direct comparison between the present "period of industrialization" and the past "period of national emancipation." The theoretical fruits of such a comparison are obvious. It would show that in a situation of dependence—under neocolonial as well as imperialist rule—the dominant social strata and their elites have not had the autonomy necessary to conduct and consummate a national revolution, and as a result ended up in a historical dead end. Nonetheless, a conclusion such as this is nothing new theoretically nor is it the fruit exclusively of this approach. We have therefore preferred a less elegant analytic and expository approach. Although at first glance historical unity may seem to have been lost, it permits a better focus on the multiple facets of the various sequences of historicosocial effects and factors related specifically to the multidimensional, constantly shifting interpenetrations of bourgeois domination and capitalist transformation. So that our exposition will not end up as a fragmentary sociological description atomizing social facts and processes into analytically independent totalities, we have chosen four strategic themes in terms of which we shall sum up our conclusions. This, we feel, is the expository approach best suited for delineating the nature and the implications of the political dilemmas that the bourgeois classes and bourgeois power have had to face in the era of the "economic miracle."[3]

Bourgeois rule and capitalist transformation

The principal theme is, of course, of a theoretical nature. It concerns the general relationship between bourgeois domination and capitalist transformation under dependent and underdeveloped capitalism in the most advanced stage of industrial growth. Thus it entails discussion of the form, nature, and functions of bourgeois domination under the concrete conditions of transition from competitive capitalism to monopoly capitalism while the dual articulation of the Brazilian economy remains intact and external imperialist domination intensifies. At this stage of the discussion, it is of no purpose to take up the utopian alternatives of the bourgeoisie, nourished ideologically from within or without (as for example the utopian belief that the spread and acceleration of industrial development would abolish "economic backwardness," eliminating, by itself, dependence and underdevelopment, i.e., destroying the dual articulation of the Brazilian economy and thereby removing precapitalist or subcapitalist forms of economic relations and imperialist domination through economic, technological, or political neutralization). In fact, a better control over "economic backwardness" does not in itself ensure the abolition of dependence and underdevelopment. It merely alters the structural conditions in which they occur, obliging bourgeois domination to adapt its form, structures, and dynamics to a kind of capitalist transformation in which the dual articulation is the rule (i.e., in which uneven internal development and imperialist domination are prerequisites for capitalist accumulation and growth). These points have been duly analyzed [in chapter 6 of *A Revolução Burguesa no Brasil*] from the sociological viewpoint followed by the author. What we must now do is to draw the right conclusions with regard to the theoretical description of bourgeois domination and its sociodynamic influences on related capitalist transformation.

The dual articulation did not merely create its own model of capitalist transformation. It also gave rise to a characteristic form of bourgeois domination, one adapted structurally, functionally, and historically to the conditions and the effects both of uneven internal development and of imperialist external domination. It is necessary to start out from this fundamental fact if we want to understand sociologically the socioeconomic aspirations and political identifications of the classes that make up the bourgeoisie in Brazil and, in particular, the way in which these classes have applied concretely their formulas for national revolution. Clearly, only the conservative polarization of bourgeois consciousness, with its "exclusivist" isolation within its own class interests and class domination, kept the national revolution from taking another road, even within capitalism. Nor is it even difficult to conceive another "possible" alternative in which the bourgeois option would take a radical turn, culminating in the simultaneous abolition of unequal internal development and external imperialist domination. However, this did not occur, aside from sporadic extremist manifestations of "revolutionary zeal" among certain factions of the bourgeois classes. When the crisis of transition had reached its peak, these classes couched their political tasks and historical mission as well as their loyalty in terms of "accelerated development" and an "institutional revolution." By this was implied the same outcome: the dimensions of national revolution would continue to be defined by the dismal organic linkage of internal uneven development and external imperialist domination.

The bourgeois classes therefore endeavored to make national revolution compatible with dependent capitalism and relative underdevelopment, assuming a "realistic" and "pragmatic" political attitude which represented a demonstration of bourgeois rationality. Does this mean, as some claim, that there has been no real national revolution, or that these classes simply betrayed the national revolution? Such judgments can be sustained, provided certain ideal prerequisites of capitalist transformation are established that do not or cannot occur at the periphery. Clearly the double articulation does not prevent national revolution; on the contrary, under dependent capitalism national revolution is just as necessary, since it constitutes the true political fulcrum of bourgeois domination and of control of the state by the bourgeoisie. But one must not lose sight of which national revolution is in question. After proposing the sorts of "development" and "revolution within the system" that were compatible with dependent capitalism, the bourgeois classes sought the only national revolution for which they could struggle under such conditions, namely the consolidation of bourgeois power through a strengthening of the national structures and functions of class domination. Therefore what mattered was not the egalitarian constraints—however formal and abstract they may have been—of a national political community, more or less complex and heterogeneous, but rather the range within which certain specific class interests could be universalized, imposed, through the state, on the entire national community, and regarded as the "interests of the nation as a whole." Thus, in the literal sense, in such a sociohistorical and political context national revolution signified horizontal integration of bourgeois class interests on a national scale and the likelihood of imposing them on the entire national community by "legitimate" and coercive means. This is the political basis of the continuity of capitalist transformation; accordingly, indirectly and over the long term it may produce consequences of some measure of utility for the other classes and of universal import as far as the dynamics of the national community are concerned. Nonetheless, the bourgeois classes do not formalize their concrete tasks in terms of such indirect relationships. Devoid of any political romanticism, "revolutionary" or "conservative," the bourgeois classes assert themselves immediately in terms of direct relationships identifying the national revolution with its own particularist goals. The empirical evidence for such an interpretation is not to be found solely in the [Brazilian] First Republic [1889-1930] and in the "institutional revolution" of 1964. Seen in the proper light, the "liberal revolution" of 1930, the Estado Novo [1937-1945], and the "nationalist developmentalist" governments of Getúlio Vargas [1950-1954] and Juscelino Kubitschek [1956-1960] traveled down the same road, although their political overtures to the base put them in a more favorable light, as if they were exceptions that confirm the rule.

The fact that the national revolution was consolidated within such a closed circle does not invalidate or limit the structural, functional, and historical significance it should have, and indeed does have, for the bourgeois classes. The crucial question for them is the national integration of a capitalist economy undergoing differentiation and growth under the conditions and influences deriving from the dual articulation of Brazil's historical situation. A comparison that is alert to the unique and crucial differences would discover that the national revolution had the same economic, social, and political importance for them as analogous revolutions had (or have) for bourgeois classes in the hegemonic capitalist nations. The national revolution aimed at consolidating bourgeois domination at the political level so as to create the political base necessary for a continuing capitalist transformation, never a simple process (because of factional conflicts within the bourgeois bloc and because of pressure from below, whether visible or not, from the laboring and destitute classes). On the other hand, thanks to its structural and dynamic links with the dual articulation, the national revolution under dependent capitalism produced a unique variety of bourgeois domination, one that organizationally and institutionally resists leveling pressures from the national structures of the established order, overcoming and even negating these impulses toward integration. A bourgeois despotism and a clear separation between civil society and nation are the result, with the bourgeois classes tending thereupon to identify bourgeois domination with a natural "revolutionary" right of absolute authority, presumably of benefit to the "active" and "enlightened" segment of civil society (all who qualify and participate in the competitive social order). The parallel tendency is to reduce the nation to an abstract entity (or a useful legal fiction), which the bourgeois classes endow with reality only in situations where they themselves happen to embody the political will of this "active" and "enlightened" minority.

In this historical and social context, bourgeois domination is not just a spontaneous socioeconomic and regulatory political force. It politically polarizes the entire network of self-defense and repression over which range the institutions linked to bourgeois power—from the press to the state—giving rise to a formidable superstructure of oppression and blockage that transforms bourgeois domination into the sole source of "legitimate political power." Only a mere reflex of the material relations of production, bourgeois domination penetrates these relations to the very core, inhibiting, suppressing, or redirecting—spontaneously as well as institutionally—the economic, social, and political processes through which the other classes or quasi-classes confront bourgeois power. This explains sociologically how and why bourgeois domination becomes a be-all and end-all not only for the continued existence of the reigning model of capitalist transformation, but for the preservation or change of its corresponding social order as well. It sets itself up as both the source and the end goal of any and all relevant social change and constitutes a barrier that effectively crushes (at least for the time being) all efforts at opposition to the prevailing bourgeois conceptions of, for example, the nature of law in a competitive society, national security, democracy, democratic education, the minimum wage, class relations, trade-union freedom, economic development, and civilization. Herein lies the source of the internal choice by the bourgeois classes of a kind of capitalism that sacrifices Brazilian society to the iniquities of uneven internal development and external imperialist domination.

It is not surprising that a sociologist should hesitate before the results of his observations and interpretations. It seems incredible that such systematic oppression can exist in our day, and moreover that it and the terrible instruments of repression to which it must resort can be reconciled with the egalitarian ideals of respect for the human person, the fundamental rights of man, and a democratic style of life. But so it is, and not just in Brazilian society at that. Variants of the same form of bourgeois domination have emerged and are being sustained and perfected in other nations of Latin America, Asia, Africa, and Europe. Leaving aside reflections that would clash with the objective spirit of sociological explication and scientific parlance, our task has been to situate the functions of this belated offshoot of the "expansion of Western civilization" and flowering of "bourgeois modernity" in the tropics.

To what economic, social, and political needs does this institutionalized machinery of class oppression respond? The direct and indirect relationships mentioned above show clearly that this form of bourgeois domination is the real key to explaining the existence and perfection of the version of capitalism that is our lot, namely *savage capitalism*. It is the "possible form of capitalism" at the periphery in an era that has seen the partitioning of the world among the hegemonic capitalist nations, the multinational corporations, and the bourgeoisies of the "developing countries" —a capitalism the permanent reality of which amounts to the wedding of capitalist development with the sumptuous life of rich and powerful bourgeois minorities and with economic prosperity in some imperialist nations, also rich and powerful; a capitalism that combines luxury, power, and wealth on the one hand with extreme poverty, despair, and oppression on the other; and finally, a capitalism in which class relationships go back to a remote past, as if the world of socially antagonistic classes were rather the worlds of distinct "nations," mutually closed and hostile to one another in a latent, implacable civil war.

Particularizing this general function, we discover three derivative functions that are key to this form of bourgeois domination. First, it is directed above all at strengthening the economic, sociocultural, and political conditions by which it maintains and renews itself, ensuring the historical continuity of the bourgeois power it contains and rendering that power as efficient as possible. Second, it is intent on amplifying the structural and dynamic incorporation of the Brazilian economy into the systems of trade, production, and finance of the hegemonic capitalist nations and the "international business community," to the end of maximizing processes of technological modernization, capitalist accumulation, and economic development, and of ensuring bourgeois power of accessible external means of support and renovation. Third, it is intent on extending and unifying the direct and indirect controls of the bourgeois classes over the state machinery so as to widen the channels between state political power and bourgeois domination and to infuse bourgeois power with a maximum of political efficiency, providing it with an institutional basis for its self-aggrandizement on a national scale.

The first two derivative functions presuppose, in the Brazilian context, a conscious and organized defense (where necessary) by the bourgeois classes in a specific form of class solidarity. This mechanically links together, in the same pattern of economic, sociocultural, and political domination, interests that are convergent and divergent, "national" capitalist and "foreign" capitalist, more or less conservative and more or less liberal, partaken of in varying measure by the high, middle, and petty bourgeoisies and by the vast numbers of foreign personnel in local subsidiaries of corporations and other foreign enterprises. The mechanical piecing together of bourgeois class solidarity has various inhibitory effects on capitalist development as well as on the spread of bourgeois domination at the economic, sociocultural, and political levels.

On the one hand, for bourgeois domination there is one and only one thing that is essential: the defense and promotion of the common interests of the national and international bourgeoisies as regards the inviolability of private property, private initiative, and bourgeois control of state political power. Divergent interests pass through the filter of mutual concessions and mutual adjustments that cancel out or drastically reduce the revolutionary impact of shifts in dominant bourgeois interests. Thus bourgeois domination interposes itself between bourgeois class antagonisms and the ferment they cause in the economic, sociocultural, and political spheres. Class unity takes on an ultraconservative tone that is easily polarized around reactionary, even profoundly reactionary, values and behavior. It requires —especially in matters in which bourgeois power takes on political connotations—the adherence of the entire bloc to what may be described as the *principia media* of bourgeois interests and values, both national and foreign. As a result, the constraining forces of bourgeois domination and the class solidarity upon which it resides stifled both bourgeois reformism (the dilemmas stemming from the agrarian reform and the expansion of the internal market are good examples) and the bourgeois democratic movement (as in the dampening of radicalization of the middle classes). The national bourgeoisie is transformed structurally into a pro-imperialist bourgeoisie incapable of moving from indirect or passive mechanisms of self-protection to actions that are straightforwardly anti-imperialistic, whether at the level of business or at the political and diplomatic levels in the strict sense.

On the other hand, this mechanical piecing together of bourgeois class solidarity inhibits the differentiation, intensification, and autonomization of internal capitalist development. Paradoxical as it may seem, certain categorical imperatives of this pattern of bourgeois domination compel the bourgeois classes to neglect or even reject certain specifically bourgeois practical tasks that would broaden the scope of the national revolution in progress as well as the meaning of the capitalist transformation itself. This neglect and neutralization of the intrinsic creative capacities of the bourgeois classes has extremely harmful consequences. The dual articulation causes various foci of precapitalist or subcapitalist development to maintain indefinitely archaic or semi-archaic socioeconomic structures, acting as an impediment to agrarian reform, the valorization of labor, the proletarianization of the worker, the expansion of the internal market, etc. It also enables speculation to develop in a context that is more quasi-colonial than purely capitalist, in all spheres of economic life (although preponderantly in the industrial and financial sector, and in urban-industrial more than agrarian capitalism). It also prevents the effectively modern or modernized economic structures from being subjected to effective social control, permitting industrial growth to continue largely subject to the old model of economic cycles, so destructive to the organic development of a capitalist economy integrated on a national scale. The absence of such effective social control enables large corporations, both national and foreign, in all branches of business, to operate with almost total freedom and allows imperialism to penetrate almost at will, wreaking its devastating effects, in every corner of Brazilian economic life. Thus, the very form of bourgeois domination corresponds to the alienation of the bourgeois classes and to the rejection of the economic, sociocultural, and political tasks incumbent on them as long as capitalist development serves to fuel the national revolution. The worst is that this is taking place at the expense of processes that will not evolve spontaneously in Brazil's particular sociohistorical situation. The effect of the dual articulation is that internal unequal development and external imperialist domination create and reinforce structural dislocations that serve to strangle capitalist transformation at its very roots. To free itself from dependent and underdeveloped capitalism, the Brazilian bourgeoisie must extract itself with utmost dispatch from the existing pattern of bourgeois domination and class solidarity, which is no more than a historical relic and as such, ready to be shelved. It should be consigned to the rubbish heap, since more than all else it is a snare, a pitfall, that takes more from the bourgeois classes than it gives. If these classes are incapable of ridding themselves of this pattern of class domination and class solidarity, it will inevitably become their tomb.

The third derivative function comprises two generally recognized sets of circumstances. One of these has to do with the political needs of self-affirmation, self-defense, and self-propagation of the various strata of the Brazilian bourgeoisie. It is not easy to steer the ship, when capitalist development has no reliable compass by which to guide the national revolution and when at one extreme of the bourgeois spectrum are to be found subcapitalist or precapitalist forms of agrarian production, at the other, "foreign multinational corporations" and "large state corporations." A convergence of interests may be obtained and even imposed, but to the detriment of bourgeois roles that have been neglected historically though hardly ever for more than short periods of time. Internal history may be disregarded where class interests and conflicts have been smothered, but the external historical rhythms of capitalism are inexorable. Hence bourgeois impotence is of a unique kind, which centers the nucleus of the bourgeoisie's power of decision making and action in the national state. What the bourgeoisie is unable to do in the private sphere, it tries to achieve through its use of the machinery, resources, and power of the state. It is this impotence, and not merely the isolation and weakness of the civil sector of the bourgeois classes that has put the state in the center of the latter-day development of capitalism in Brazil; furthermore, it explains why that sector has been repeatedly drawn into alliances with the military, invariably militarizing the state and the political administrative structure, in all our "crises" since the proclamation of the Republic. The pattern of class domination and class solidarity we have described has facilitated such a constellation, with the bourgeois classes forging an alliance among themselves on a higher level and thereby transforming impotence into its opposite, into a force that has been relatively uncontrollable (at least by the other classes and by external imperialist pressures). Thus, the national state is neither a contingent nor even a secondary actor in this system of bourgeois domination. It is its very essence and, indeed, it is the state alone which is able to pave the bitter road for the bourgeois classes to a national revolution, prolonged by the contradictions of dependent capitalism and underdevelopment.

The second set of circumstances regards the possibility of

preserving the existing bourgeois order. The bourgeois classes' dissensions, which are diverse and deep enough to require a mechanism of class unity and solidarity such as we have described, and the pressure from below, which is quite strong despite the seeming "apathy" of the proletarian, rural working, and destitute classes and has required the suppression of all means of self-assertion by these classes, must be kept from destroying the precarious existing economic, social, and political equilibrium. Even here state power emerges as the framework and driving mechanism of bourgeois power. If it had not absorbed this power and the bottleneck it caused in the functions of the state, bourgeois domination would have vanished like a breeze. In dependent and underdeveloped capitalism, bourgeois domination cannot keep itself going, compel obeisance, and crush class conflicts by relying exclusively on private means of class domination and on the conventional functions of the democratic-bourgeois state. Thus, in its recent evolution, the Brazilian national state has been molded by the needs and interests of the bourgeois classes and, in particular, by the peculiar interweaving of their system of class domination with the control of a dependent and underdeveloped capitalist economy and class society. Insofar as these classes have been able to restrain and unify their own demands, by grouping around common or meshing internal and external capitalist interests, they have been able to silence and exclude the other classes from the struggle for state power, creating ideal conditions for bending the state to their own collective private ends. Aside from the other conditions favorable to this end, which will be discussed later on, the authoritarian nature of presidentialism, and the strong loyalty to bourgeois domination on the part of the military, who profoundly and stubbornly identify with bourgeois aims, have made it extremely easy to domesticate the state to subserve parochial interests. Clearly, the militarization of the structures and functions of the national state simplified and reinforced this whole process, so that in the end the linkage of bourgeois domination and an open and institutionalized class dictatorship achieved an efficiency that would never have been possible within a conventional democratic bourgeois state. Still, the bourgeois order remained amply vulnerable in its association with dependent and underdeveloped capitalism. Bourgeois domination was merely made more efficient, within the limitations of the historical conditions. In fact, the bourgeois classes themselves have a clear social perception of the significance of the aforementioned arrangements. They are instrumental: they adapt bourgeois power to the conditions, stable and unstable, of a national revolution that has been continually battered by uneven internal development and external imperialist domination. Over the long term, the alternative is obvious. Either bourgeois domination establishes itself on a new foundation, adapting to pressures from below and to the "dialogue between the classes," or it is doomed to vanish even sooner.

This description of the nature, forms, and functions of bourgeois domination in Brazilian society, though summary, still throws light on the essentials. It describes a particular evolution, since it focuses on the bourgeois classes, domination, and power in a specific society. Nonetheless, this evolution is also typical: it displays the interaction between bourgeois domination and capitalist transformation at the periphery. It shows how dependent and underdeveloped capitalism is a creation of bourgeoisies who are compelled to make use of the immense material, institutional, and human resources at hand and the civilization placed at their disposal by capitalism, to limit the national revolution to their narrow class interests and values. For this reason they stifle those familiar bourgeois impulses toward egalitarianism, reformism, and extreme nationalism, purging them from the competitive social order by all means, both peaceful and violent. At the same time, they foment and intensify other equally familiar impulses, toward accumulative and expropriative rationality, individualism, exclusivism, and class despotism, using means both peaceful and violent to ensure their predominance in the historical elaboration of the competitive social order. In a word, they become the builders, perpetuators, and transformers of dependent and underdeveloped capitalism, bringing modernization to the periphery and adapting bourgeois domination to the functions it must assume if capitalist transformation is not only to reproduce itself under very special conditions but also to be able structurally and dynamically to keep pace with the historical rhythms of the central and hegemonic capitalist economies.

Protracted counter-revolution and the "acceleration of history"

This discussion suggests a question, bringing us to the second theme of the present discussion: namely, how can one explain sociologically the relative success of the Brazilian bourgeoisie in this movement, which in the end led it to recognize and carry out the tasks and roles incumbent on it within the global historical context? Answers to this question generally stress four factors: (1) the demographic, economic, and social characteristics of Brazilian society, which made a renewed upsurge of industrialism and the acceleration of economic growth with external collaboration both easy and viable; (2) the intensive technological, economic, and political assistance of the hegemonic capitalist nations and the "international business community"; (3) the strong identification of the armed forces with the economic, social, and political impulses of the bourgeois classes and their crucial practical role in the rearticulation of the composite pattern of bourgeois domination; (4) the ambiguity of democratic bourgeois reformist and nationalist movements and the weakness of the revolutionary socialist movement, with its pervasive petit bourgeois element and low level of popular or working-class participation. Indeed these factors are sufficient to explain "what happened," but they confine the answers to the morphological aspects of class relations and conflicts. It is possible to go further, investigating why, in the final analysis, at a particular moment the Brazilian bourgeoisie took a historical turn that was specifically counter-revolutionary in terms of the "classic" democratic bourgeois model of national revolution and involved a break with the entire ideological and utopian arsenal inherent in the "republican tradition" of that bourgeoisie. With this we enter the domain of class consciousness and collective class behavior, which unfortunately have been little and poorly investigated. However, if we confine ourselves to a few general observations, we can venture a reply to this question at the most important explanatory level.

The four decades following World War I comprise the crucial period of the historical maturation of the Brazilian bourgeoisie. This period does not represent, as many believe, its "formative epoch" (as we have seen, this happened much earlier); nor, as others maintain, does it correspond to the "period of oligarchic crisis," since in Brazil this crisis took the form of a reshuffling of inherited economic, social, and political structures, whereby the oligarchic social strata, ancient or recent, were reabsorbed by the class society in the process of constitution and expansion. Thus there was no true displacement of the dominant "old class" or "old classes" by dominant "new classes" of contemporary origin.

What took place was much broader and more dramatic, even though it did not appear so: namely, the structural coalescence of different social strata and different economic groupings that made up the "possessing classes," increasingly identified with a bourgeois outlook and a bourgeois style of life, by dint of the rapid and continuing acceleration of the urban commercial revolution and then of industrialization. The dominant estates of the "*ancien régime*" were thus integrated into the structures of the competitive social order and the class society in process of formation or expansion (depending on the part of the country). The "traditional" or "modern" oligarchies were nonetheless affected very little by all this and their crisis of reabsorption did not have the same significance as did the appearance of the bourgeoisie as a sociohistorical category and a political community.

This is the principal historical fact of this period. A far-ranging process of socialization of economic, social, and political power was set into motion through which the bourgeois social classes were able to forge a unity on the basis of their material interests, style of life, and outlook. Initially, the predominance of agrocommercial interests posed certain obstacles to this process; nonetheless, the 1930 revolution shows that it was already far advanced, long before industrial and financial interests attained the relative predominance that they achieved under the Estado Novo and, in particular, during and after World War II. The bourgeoisie, which had been a social residuum and later an atomized stratum dispersed throughout Brazilian society, lost in the intermediate estates and slavishly imitative of the aristocracy, finally acquired a distinct physiognomy, establishing itself as an organized social force occupying the summit of class society, where it functioned as its chief political, cultural, and socioeconomic driving force. But it is one thing to view this process as an accomplished fact. It is another to focus on it at each of the stages passed through by the economic, sociocultural, and political agglomeration of the various bourgeois classes and class strata in their process of horizontal integration on a national scale. For these classes and their various substrata to achieve a true bourgeois type of class solidarity, which would enable them to integrate horizontally and on a national scale their material interests and collective behavior and to join ranks in a unified political community, they had first to undergo a complex and difficult transformation. Specifically, it was necessary for them to divest themselves of the "second human nature" that slavery had impressed upon the "possessing classes"; to make a concerted effort to revise and redefine the ideologies and utopias taken from European and North American democratic bourgeois experience and from the epoch of national emancipation; and finally, to achieve an understanding of their own reality in terms of the historical roles and tasks they might perform as the bourgeoisie of an underdeveloped and dependent class society in the era of monopoly capitalism and total imperialism.

This meant a revolution extremely complicated and difficult, not because of the oligarchic element itself, but because it was necessary to extract the bourgeois ethos from the patrimonialist web in which it was entangled as a result of almost four centuries of the tradition of slavery and a coarse commercial capitalism. On the other hand, the fragmentation of the bourgeois classes and class strata was much more propititious to their local or regional isolation and atomization than to the horizontal unification on a national scale, of interests and values but vaguely and moreover predominantly locally perceived. The rustic character of most of the cities, the tenuous penetration of urban life into the countryside, and the patchiness of processes of cultural secularization and rationalization of the overall bourgeois understanding of the world aggravated this phenomenon, prolonging the stage of quasi-class and semi-class existence of the bourgeois strata, deprived as they were of the chief external factors responsible for spreading and shaping the *bourgeois cast of mind* (or to use a better expression, the bourgeois *cultural horizon*). To all this must be added the weakness, numerically, economically, and politically, of the middle sectors, steeped in a strong traditionalism and displaying a contradictory ambivalence in their attitudes, deriving from resentments partly psychological, partly social (and not from social impulses of a reformist or revolutionary nature); and finally the belated and at the same time very slow appearance of the typical "modern entrepreneur" on a mass scale in high commerce, industry, and finance. In a word, a series of elements converged to incline the bourgeois classes toward a false bourgeois consciousness, maintaining among these classes and throughout the rest of society illusions that did even greater violence to the bourgeois ideologies imported from Europe and the United States. These illusions had always been nourished and disseminated by a broad range of spokesmen (as for example the Republican propagandists, the Modernists, the *Tenentes*, the constitutionalists, the nationalists, etc.*). One could say that the "notables" of the bourgeoisie made these illusions into their political credo, establishing them as a kind of *mores* of Brazilian civilization. In turn, the popular masses and the young were attracted by these illusions, which opened false reformist and democratic prospects for national revolution. However, the development of capitalism within Brazil did not carry bourgeois society in that direction. It did not produce a "heroic" "conquistador" bourgeoisie, nor was it able to further any kind of bourgeois egalitarianism, reformism, or fanatical nationalism. To "govern their world" the bourgeois classes had first to get to know it better and instill bourgeois rationality into what they understood as their historical roles in dependent capitalism.

This apprenticeship evolved in stages, and along three different paths, all frustrating. First, through the discovery that we would not "repeat history": the great Republican hope that the industrial revolution would come about autonomously, following the model of competitive capitalist economic development, crumbled to dust at the very threshold of intensive industrialization. This became clear at the very time it was realized that the concrete institution of a full-fledged bourgeois democracy was neither a "question of time" nor one of "political gradualism." All these calculations and expectations had to be revised. The Brazilian bourgeoisie learned at one stroke that history does not produce itself; and that it does not correct human errors, whether arising from exaggerated ambitions or commonplace fantasies. Second, a series of clashes took place, fueled by the divergent interests and aspirations of the bourgeois classes or their various substrata. Ignorant of the limits of their historical roles, civil or military sectors of the high and middle bourgeoisie at various times embarked upon adventures that were labeled "nationalist," "democratic," and "revolutionary" and indeed were actually intended as such. They would have been so as well if it had been possible first to transform the dependent foundations of the relations of production and the market. Nonetheless, the bourgeois classes who were struggling for such broad causes did not have the courage to break with imperialist domination or with the shackles that bound

---

*The Modernists—a cultural movement of the 1920s approximating Futurism and Art Deco in style, centered in Sao Paulo. The *Tenentes*—army lieutenants, in fact junior officers, who led rebellions against the government in the 1920s. The reference to constitutionalists and nationalists is more generally applicable to political positions than to movements. —Ed.

them to various forms of internal underdevelopment. As a consequence, they patronized a peculiar variety of "populism," *populist demagogy*, which aggravated class conflicts without broadening the democratic, reformist, and nationalist space of the bourgeois political order. These were nevertheless experiences that brought the Brazilian bourgeoisie to an awareness of its true condition, teaching it not to seek relative advantages for isolated strata of the bourgeoisie at the cost of its overall collective security and the stability of bourgeois domination. Third, the elite of the bourgeois classes was exposed to external socializing influences and direct internal manipulation by means of controls activated or directed from without. As competitive capitalism passed into monopoly capitalism, imperialist domination intensified. In monopoly capitalism there are no bounds set on the external control of a society: imperialism is, so to speak, total.

Experiences in this area are well known. Groups plucked from various professional civil and military levels were shipped abroad, where they underwent a total recycling (ideological and utopian) in programs of "training," "specialization," and "indoctrination." Mass propaganda is disseminated via radio, television, the press, and even in the schools, and there are technical aid programs—public health, military cooperation, public safety, economic assistance, cooperation in education, etc.—that are elaborate networks of "directed modernization." Finally, there are the programs of the international and intergovernmental institutions in these and other areas, all spreading a specific developmentalist philosophy. In Brazil the bourgeois strata have learned to alter their global perceptions and interpretations so as to adjust themselves to "pragmatic assessments" that portray underdevelopment as a "normal" fact that will correct itself, and set forth the principle, put into circulation by the United States, of "development with security" as a fundamental ideal. Thus the Brazilian bourgeoisie found new pathways of "modernization." It abandoned its historical libertarian paraphernalia of European origin, and replaced them with beliefs that were a good deal more prosaic but nevertheless adjusted the roles of the bourgeoisie to "hemispheric unity," "the interdependence of democratic nations," and the "defense of Western civilization." To get a concrete picture of how these three paths of apprenticeship altered the perception of reality and the values of the Brazilian bourgeoisie we need only follow the recent political or administrative careers of some of the "rebel" civil and military leaders of the twenties, thirties, and forties. It is strange to see how, among many of the representatives of "nationalist," "democratic," and "revolutionary" bourgeois currents, "oligarchic mentality" came into correspondence with "pragmatic rationalism" as the expurgation of bourgeois idealism was completed.

The hegemonic nations obviously export their ideologies and utopias, and insofar as they do these are also the ideologies and utopias of the dominant classes in the dependent nations. But one must remember that this takes place within a framework delimited by different economic, sociohistorical, and political conditions. The dependent capitalist nations do not have the same capacities. The ideologies and utopias of their ruling classes are no longer under effective social control, since frequently the other classes do not have a bargaining position or means of self-defense "within the order." On the other hand, these ideologies and utopias very often lose their utility, in most cases becoming a source of rationalization and legitimation of the advantages the ruling classes routinely derive from their compliant submission to external interests and manipulation. Thus, the same thing that happened with liberalism happened later with developmentalism and the catastrophic doctrine of "strong democracy," albeit under quite different conditions. The renovation of the ideas, values, and behavioral patterns of the bourgeois classes and their substrata augmented the general perception and critical awareness, in the "realistic" and "pragmatic" sense, of the overall situation and how it meshed with bourgeois class interests, whether threatened or not. But it made no definite contribution to an improvement or broadening of the identification of these classes and their substrata with the everyday social dilemmas of the poor or with what may be described euphemistically as the "general interests of the whole nation." On the contrary, the new kind of "controlled modernization" tended to shift sentiment away from loyalty to the nation and the ideological or utopian polarizations of national revolution, and toward a loyalty to certain very abstract and supranational causes such as "hemispheric solidarity," "solidarity with the democratic nations," or "defense of Christian and Western civilization." Thus the internationalization of the material structures of the relations of production and the market visibly extended to the superstructures of the relations of bourgeois power. Accordingly the bourgeoisies at the periphery experienced an ideological and utopian

vacillation induced and guided from without. Classes champion-
ing the national democratic bourgeois revolution began to see
themselves as pillars of the world order of capitalism, of "democracy," and of "Christian civilization." In its internal repercussions,
this ideological and utopian about-face compounded the philosophical, historical, and political alienation of the bourgeoisie
from national problems and their solutions. It also heightened
their insensitivity to them so long as they did not disturb internal
capitalist development or the "stability of the world capitalist system" or, further, so long as they were useful for intensifying capitalist accumulation. It also fostered a vast indulgence toward attitudes and behaviors that clashed head-on with the *mores* of democracy and Christian civilization, thereby indirectly broadening
the psychological, cultural, and political license for a class freedom
that was extremely egoistical and irresponsible. At bottom, this
about-face provided a new psychological, moral, and political basis
for a rigidified bourgeois rule and its transformation into an overtly authoritarian and totalitarian social force.

Here, and not in any supposed deterioration of liberalism or
presumed recrudescence of traditionalist authoritarianism, are to
be found the psychosocial and historical roots of the shift in the
cultural horizon of the bourgeois classes and their various substrata. This shift has led gradually over the last four decades to a
political philosophy and to class actions that laid their primary
emphasis on securing the privileged status of bourgeois interests as
a whole. It has thus served as a foundation for a class solidarity
that ceased being "democratic" or even authoritarian, and became
overtly "totalitarian" and counter-revolutionary. In a word, it provided the leavening for the emergence of a *preventive* class dictatorship.

There is no denying that this change enabled the bourgeois
classes and their substrata to take a truly historical leap and effec-
tuate their own horizontal integration on a national scale directly
at the level of class rule, even before the process of vertical differentiation was completed. On the other hand, this change also enabled them to extract strategic advantages from conflicts that were
undermining bourgeois solidarity from within, and from conflicts
with the working and impoverished classes. The first point explains why they were able to abandon their customary temporiz-
ing and gradualism so rapidly and with such facility. By carrying
through their own horizontal integration, at least at the level of

class rule, they were able to impose their own interests on the other classes and on the nation as a whole. Whatever the disadvantages of consolidation on the basis of common interests or, conversely, of an accommodation of disparate and heterogeneous interests, it did not entail political risks. *In fine*, the model ensuing from a collective and compound bourgeois hegemony was less of an evil than the "defeat of the nation"—i.e., the disintegration of the bourgeois order and the collapse of bourgeois power.

The second point explains how the bourgeois classes and their substrata exploited to their own advantage both internal social conflicts and their conflicts with the proletariat, the working classes in general, and the marginal or excluded classes. Factional conflicts redounded exclusively to the advantage of the bourgeoisie, instead of serving as a basis for stimulating the much touted "structural reforms," an intensifying of the national revolution, or possible "openings" toward the democratization of wealth and power. The conflicts with the antagonistic classes were stigmatized, situated "outside of the system," and throttled by repressive and violent measures, and hence were disconnected from the democratic bourgeois national revolution. Once again it was the bourgeoisie which benefited. In the name of "defending the stability of the system," therefore, the bourgeois classes and their substrata took advantage of these conflicts to legitimize the transformation of bourgeois domination into a preventive class dictatorship and to invest with privilege their own real power, which the bourgeoisie derived from its class domination as if it were an embodiment of the "legitimately established" order. The bourgeois nation came thus to prevail over the legal nation. But the bourgeoisie was prepared to accept this dislocation in the system (in reality a counter-revolution which included recourse to civil war) as necessary in order to safeguard "legality," the "democratic order," and the "interests of the People."

Our interpretation has sought to avoid certain distortions that bourgeois radicalism, reformist socialism, and even a mechanistic revolutionary socialism have introduced in the analysis of the bourgeois revolution in capitalist countries at the periphery. We have not sought to describe the relations of bourgeois domination to capitalist transformation as a function of presumed "universal determinants." We have thus also avoided the false correlative problem of "why did history not repeat itself?" To these two interpretive approaches we have contrasted a search for the specific links between bourgeois domination and capitalist transformation where uneven internal development and external imperialist domination are permanent intrinsic realities despite all the quantitative and qualitative changes that capitalism may undergo.

Like its own social scientists or its socialist or communist adversaries, the Brazilian bourgeoisie was ignorant of what may be called the "harsh reality" of its condition throughout a considerable period—at least as long as it did not have to face the problems created by intensive industrialization and as long as internal underdevelopment and external imperialist domination were maintained. But as soon as it began to confront these problems and, in particular, when it then saw its capacity for survival in the face of these problems directly threatened, the Brazilian bourgeoisie had to carry out a Copernican revolution in both its cultural horizon and its political sphere. This was what we have tried, however briefly, to sketch within the perspective chosen, describing how the bourgeoisie became aware of its situation and tried to divest itself, in the domains of economic, social, and political action, of utopian illusions of bourgeois democracy and bourgeois nationalism. The external transformations in the rhythms and structures of world capitalism and imperialism further aggravated the exacting problems of this bourgeoisie, forcing it to realize that it could not sustain capitalist transformation if it broke its dual articulation. Indeed, it had to do the opposite, linking the internal factors of capitalist accumulation ever more firmly with the uneven development of the Brazilian economy and the enslaving dynamics of the multinational corporations, the hegemonic capitalist nations, and world capitalism.

Nonetheless, the breaks that had to be made were as drastic as cutting off an arm or a leg. What is the fate of a bourgeoisie that destroys the ideological and utopian image which was to its liking and which it has a compensatory need to absorb historically? The drama is at once psychological, moral, and political. It begins as a historical dilemma, and ends as a tremendous political challenge. To break the Gordian knot it was necessary to divest bourgeois domination of all effective ties that were substantively and effectively bourgeois-democratic and bourgeois-nationalist, by neutralizing specifically democratic and nationalist pressures from the radical bourgeois sectors and by quashing pressures for economic, social, and political equality, for national integration, or for the mobilization of the popular masses on a class basis. Once the leap was made in this direction, the extent of the success achieved would determine how far this bourgeoisie could go in its new historical adjustment to dependent capitalism now in the era of monopoly capitalism and total imperialism. Therefore, at the root of the crisis of bourgeois power was the historico-social necessity for the Brazilian bourgeoisie to adapt to industrialism, not in an evolutionary process that would intensify national revolution, as occurred in competitive capitalism, but, on the contrary, which would aggravate uneven internal development and intensify external imperialist domination, since both were, irremediably, the flesh and bones and nerves of intensive industrialism. With this crisis surmounted, the Brazilian bourgeoisie became a "mature bourgeoisie," capable of undertaking intensive industrialization as a higher and more complex stage of capitalist transformation, and of consummating the bourgeois revolution, albeit under the conditions and within the context of dependent capitalism. In fact, the crisis did not tend toward autonomous national capitalist development or autonomous national revolution, nor could it, given the terms of the Brazilian bourgeoisie's class interest. Rather, the outcome of the crisis was to establish the bourgeois classes and their substrata as an autonomous force within Brazilian class society and to enable them to complete and consummate the capitalist transformation without eliminating the situation of dependence and the effects it regularly exerted on the country's relative underdevelopment.

Although the relative historical success achieved by the Brazilian bourgeoisie does have a structural basis—the horizontal integration of bourgeois class power and its impact on bourgeois consciousness, bourgeois class solidarity, and bourgeois domination—its practical effectiveness is only short-term. It has not brought about any sort of "lasting stabilization" of the bourgeois order, nor could it have, since it was a broad historical process. Nonetheless, it has furnished, and will continue to furnish for some time, the conditions necessary for the bourgeois classes and their substrata to work out and implement a comprehensive policy that will have structural and dynamic effects over the middle and long term. Thus bourgeois power is in the process, now and in the near future, of achieving the immediate objectives that had brought on the crisis in the first place and required a reorganization of the bourgeois order along autocratic, authoritarian, and totalitarian lines.

Nevertheless, even in the Brazilian situation it is almost certain that the transformations brought about by the hardening of bourgeois domination and the imposition of a preventive bourgeois class dictatorship do not belong to the category of things that have "come to stay." Nothing "comes to stay" in history, much less in the history of a regime as unstable as a class regime. The Brazilian bourgeoisie can therefore only reckon with an "armed peace" that will last as long as the presently articulated composite pattern of bourgeois domination is able to resist the counter-pressures of bourgeois radicalism, the popular masses, and the proletariat. Over the long term these will reconstitute themselves, grow, and become stronger by dint of the new sociohistorical conditions brought about by intensive industrialization and monopoly capitalism. Once the process of "bourgeois counter-revolution" reached its climax, it seemed that this pattern of class domination would not last more than one or two decades (even though it had lasted almost a half a century in countries such as Portugal and Spain). At that time it was presumed that bourgeois radicalism would easily resume its course under economic, social, and political conditions even more propitious to the recrudescence of revolutionary nationalism and bourgeois democracy. On the other hand, it was also supposed that the popular masses and the proletariat would overcome relatively soon their political suppression, and block the stigmatization of their social and political movements and the political compression of their egalitarian demands. However, similar developments in Latin America and elsewhere have demonstrated that the bourgeois autocratic movement was an alternative that could count on a quite strong and steady external reinforcement. In the light of this circumstance, the duration of preventive bourgeois dictatorships is contingent on dynamic forces capable of achieving much greater efficiency and continuity than native bourgeoisies at the periphery would, if left to their own means, be able to impart to the process. Nonetheless, we should bear in mind that class society itself generates tensions and conflicts, both pro- and anti-bourgeois, uninterruptedly, subjecting it constantly to self-disintegration. This tendency reappears at the periphery where it achieves even greater dimensions because of uneven internal development and its sociopathic effects, direct and indirect. The means of oppression and repression at the disposal of bourgeois domination in Brazil, even under the quite special conditions following upon the political hardening and militarization of the state, are not sufficient to "eternalize" something that is in essence (as well as in terms of the strategy of the national and international bourgeoisie itself) of a transient nature. From this perspective, despite its impressive magnitude, the historical achievement of the bourgeoisie is limited to surmounting the immediate disturbances caused by the crisis of bourgeois power, making it a real two-edged sword in all respects.

The political structure of the bourgeois autocracy

The third theme of the present discussion has to do with the internal political structure of the autocratic bourgeois model of capitalist transformation. Obviously this structure does not, in sociological terms, reflect just the economic, sociocultural, and political conditions of the present state of Brazilian class society under a quite robust dependent and underdeveloped capitalism. At the same time it reflects the political objectives and designs, some deliberate some less so, that have motivated the practical actions of the bourgeois classes and their substrata in the already described crisis of bourgeois power in Brazil. It also reflects both the chances that these objectives and designs will be effectively incorporated in the processes of social stability and change specific to class society, and the degree of rationality displayed by the bourgeois classes and their substrata in taking advantage of the political space accruing from these processes. Finally, it reveals the way in which directly and indirectly political interests transmitted by the dynamics of the hegemonic capitalist nations, the multinational corporations, and the international business community meshed with these designs and objectives and with their "historical possibilities," reinforcing them and hence enhancing their viability over the short and long term. We are unable here to go into all the aspects of such a vast and complex subject, which deserves a special study and even a whole book in itself. We shall only be concerned with the minimal political requirements and implications, which will situate and explain sociologically, in our view, the concrete historical form of the autocratic bourgeois model of capitalist transformation and how it evolved, totally altering, at least for the time being, the purport and consequences of class relations and conflicts.

The adaptation of bourgeois domination to the emergent historical conditions of intensive industrialization, metropolitanization of the large cities, and the development of monopoly capitalism was accompanied by the multiplication and exacerbation of social conflicts and antagonisms, chronically eroding and hence jeopardizing bourgeois power. A prerevolutionary situation of the sort rooted in the anti-bourgeois rebellion of the wage-earning and impoverished classes never came into being. Nevertheless, the situation was potentially prerevolutionary, considering the extent to which bourgeois domination was disintegrating, losing its bearings, and in general coming apart at the seams. Indeed, from the second decade of the century to the "institutional revolution" of 1964 it had been exposed without surcease to a steady process of erosion from within. The lines of cleavage formed within and outside the bourgeoisie. The bourgeois classes and their substrata wrangled among themselves over varied conflicting interests that could easily have been reconciled had the unification and centralization of bourgeois power come about more quickly (especially at the institutional level, and in particular in the conduct of the trade associations, the political parties, and the state). The internecine conflicts posed no threat to the survival of bourgeois domination and bourgeois power. However, since they were not promptly resolved they blocked the sociodynamic potential of bourgeois domination and the political effectiveness of bourgeois power, which was chronically atomized and wavering. Both grew as a static effect of the expansion of the capitalist economy and the class regime (a part of this effect being the low level of anti-bourgeois political response among the urban and rural wage-earning classes). The bourgeois and pro-bourgeois forces directly invested with state political power or involved in channeling its application were barely involved in spontaneous and deliberate political articulation. On the other hand, the conflicts that were tolerated and contained "within the order" grew steadily worse, to a large extent as a consequence of this inhibition and paralysis of bourgeois domination and bourgeois power. Various strata of the high bourgeoisie attacked each other, defending economic policies or privileges, while the middle sectors converted their frustrations and aspirations into factors that dissociated bourgeois radicalism from the existing and possible bourgeois order. As a consequence, it was the bourgeois classes and their substrata who created the rifts by which political instability was installed at the center of class conflicts, often with the intent of stirring up to their own advantage the pro-bourgeois or anti-bourgeois radicalism of the popular masses, in particular, of the urban proletariat and rural workers. Although at no time did this "pressure from within the order" ever go beyond bourgeois concerns, it did fragment the bourgeoisie, while at the same time impeding a faster centralization of bourgeois power taking place then, either directly or via the centralization of the political power of the state. Thus various areas of permanent dissension took on definition, around which gravitated the projects of national revolution; as a result the bourgeois classes and their substrata were unable to come to any basic accord regarding common interests and goals. Throughout this long period, these classes and their substrata learned more "what they should not do" so as not to undercut their situation irremediably than "what they should do" to articulate their class interests into a political community.

The internal expansion of the capitalist economy and the class regime ultimately generated a political pressure strong enough to arouse and foster bourgeois class solidarity. First, the "pressures within the order" through which the bourgeois classes and their substrata attempted to protect themselves and solidify their privileges went beyond bourgeois limits and pro-bourgeois identifications. The democratic and nationalist impulses inherent in bourgeois radicalism and in displays of "populist demagogy," directed and cultivated by relatively "enlightened" and "rebellious" sectors of the bourgeoisie, went beyond the reformism and democratic bourgeois nationalism compatible with the relatively weak equilibrium of the dependent and underdeveloped class society. The extreme social concentration of wealth and power did not provide the bourgeoisie with political room in which to maneuver and connect with other more or less divergent social interests. It could make a show of being "democratic," "reformist," and "nationalist," only so long as the "pressures within the order" remained merely symbolic of moral and political identification, devoid of real impact on historical events. In a word, the bourgeois classes and their substrata were unable to make use of bourgeois radicalism to capture the sympathy and support of the popular masses without at the same time deepening conflicts among themselves and—what was more important—without jeopardizing the material and political foundations of the competitive social order of dependent and underdeveloped capitalism. The emergence and spread of anti-bourgeois mass movements in the cities and even in some areas of the countryside, though far from representing an "immediate danger," at least in and by themselves, were unsettling and showed an unexpected tendency to spread. Hence they ended by stirring up bourgeois radicalism to an almost incontrollable pitch. These movements "contaminated" students, intellectuals, priests, the military, various sectors of the petite bourgeoisie, etc. Moreover, overtly anti-bourgeois and revolutionary influences filtered down to the masses, who were aroused yet held in check by "populist demagogy," setting up dangerous connections between poverty, "pressure within the order," and social upheaval.

Second, the state, unabashedly interventionist, because of the extreme differentiation and compacted growth of its direct economic and many cultural functions, was transformed into a formidable administrative machine (on account of its corps of functionaries and technicians) and a considerable socioeconomic force (on account of the multitude of state corporations and special government programs). The bourgeoisie invariably undermined this process. Nevertheless it depended on it and was forced to accept and encourage it, while at the same time trying to keep the state and its economic, cultural, and political forces contained within the sphere of bourgeois power. In this the bourgeoisie was assisted by the direct and indirect political effects of uneven internal development and by the presidency in a country whose legislative and judiciary branches are condemned to be dominated by conservative bourgeois or pro-bourgeois interests. The dimensions attained by the Brazilian state as an administrative and political organization, and the flooding of bourgeois radicalism into state power through the politics pursued by certain populist administrations and through the nationalist identification that came into fashion among high-level functionaries and technicians, soon aroused new fears. The state became a kind of monster, not in itself (the "populist" administrations and the "top-level" nationalist bureaucracy did not dare go too far) but because of what this shift appeared to represent, namely a loss of bourgeois control over the state, in addition to its apparent negative consequences for private initiative and bourgeois freedom. The recent patrimonialist past of the Brazilian bourgeoisie, its aggressive parochialism, and its arrogant conservative authoritarianism barred a broader, more flexible understanding of the problem such as, by way of exception, Roberto Simonsen and the exponents of "industrialism" had championed as this process was getting off the ground. The mere setting up of institutional autonomy for the basic functions of the state seemed to threaten a real nationalization of the state's administrative and political structures and an independent centralization of power, thus appearing to be a clear and ominous anti-bourgeois "revolution within the order." In fact, had such a political transformation come about, the bourgeoisie would have lost control of the state. Various political processes stemming from "pressure from within the order" were gradually transformed into their opposites, becoming factors in "a revolution within the order" against which the bourgeois classes and their substrata could do little or nothing without the repressive and oppressive institutional support they had always gotten from the state. Bourgeois power would have dwindled to nothing had it lost its monopoly over state power, and this threat even began to haunt bourgeois groups gravitating toward bourgeois radicalism and "populist" demagogy.

Third, intensive industrialization and the development of monopoly capitalism intensified, convulsively, the external influences on internal capitalist development, requiring the bourgeois classes and their substrata to find new ways of accommodating and controlling these influences. It was impossible to check the process, engendered by the worldwide structure of capitalism and spurred by the dependent nature of the Brazilian capitalist economy. The bourgeois classes and substrata nevertheless still had to deal with its political effects. Whereas the penetration of competitive capitalism from without did not directly affect the structures of political power in Brazil, such was not the case with monopoly capitalism. This class and its substrata suddenly found themselves the antagonists of their principal ally, and the "foreign challenge" also arose, like a bogeyman. As a measure of self-defense and self-assertion by "private initiative," efforts were undertaken to expand ties with "external capital," stimulating foreign investment and thus controlled modernization from without. Meanwhile, the need of the Brazilian bourgeoisie to protect itself as a class set a limit to "interdependence." Beyond the inflow of capital, technique, and firms, and even beyond the acceleration of capitalist development, the bourgeoisie still had its *status*, part intermediary, part free, of a "national" bourgeoisie. The real internal power of the bourgeoisie as regards dependent and underdeveloped capitalism and the connections between the national capitalist economies of the periphery and the hegemonic capitalist nations and world capitalist system turned on this *status*. The bourgeois classes and their substrata found themselves having to safeguard it, although at close range they were engaged in a pro-imperialist crusade. If that status were impugned, there would be no material basis for the native bourgeoisie to assert itself as part of a national system of power. It would automatically cease to be a "national" bourgeoisie, although it would still be dependent and at the periphery of the capitalist world, and would revert to the condition of "buffer" bourgeoisie, typical of colonial and neocolonial economies on the road to capitalism and national emancipation (the best example of which is the Chinese "comprador" bourgeoisie). It is quite clear, therefore, how important this status is for a dependent bourgeoisie: it constitutes the material basis for its self-defense in the context of the international relations of the world capitalist system. Deprived of this status, the indigenous bourgeoisies at the periphery could not count on the support and political functions which the state monopoly of power confers and which they need to survive as an economic community; hence the political travail of the "foreign challenge" for a bourgeoisie so bent on bringing about the capitalist transformation by means of external collaboration and ties with foreign capital.

These three sources of direct and indirect pressure converged to impart to the crisis of bourgeois power a catastrophic political significance and to compel the bourgeois classes and their substrata to seek class unity, however precarious, in their common political and material interests. The question was no longer even to gain time, putting off repeatedly the confrontation with reality, but rather to utilize the domination and power of the bourgeoisie as active elements in their political self-defense and self-assumed political privilege. In short, it was necessary to conjure up the bogeymen, real or imaginary, that troubled the gilded dreams of the bourgeois classes and their substrata, and to trigger a real battle for the "bourgeois world" that appeared to be so threatened.

Some of the points we have focused on in this extremely brief outline of events should be kept carefully in mind since they are typical of the organization and functioning of class society in dependent and underdeveloped capitalism (they do not take the same form where the bourgeois revolution follows the "classical," liberal democratic course). We are referring to the social reaction, tempered, of course, by the interests and values of the dominant bourgeois classes, to the "pressures within the system" and the "pressures against the system," and to the manipulation of these two kinds of pressures by the bourgeois classes and their substrata.

Without any "sociological idealization," it is clear that where the democratic bourgeois model of capitalist transformation found fertile historical soil there prevailed a broad correspondence among bourgeois radicalism, reformism, and "pressures within the system" originating in the urban and rural proletariat or among the masses. The class situation of the bourgeoisie withstood this correspondence since its material basis of class power was sufficiently integrated, stable, and secure to permit, and even to require, the free manifestation of those dynamic economic, social, and political forces which only the wage-earning classes could set into motion. As a consequence, bourgeois radicalism in the end reflected—structurally, functionally, and ideologically—pressures from labor, the proletariat, or trade unions which quite often went beyond and collided with specifically bourgeois class interests. All this often made the relationship between bourgeois radicalism and reformist socialism ambiguous (and even fostered what Lenin called a "bourgeois infection" of Marxism). On the other hand, the "pressures against the system" were tolerated at the ideological level and even in practice, being objectified socially in the trade-union movement, workers' parties, etc. The relationship of these pressures to bourgeois radicalism was also unquestionably highly ambiguous and complex. Bourgeois radicalism was able to advance far enough to absorb at least those pressures that were compatible with those kinds of "revolution within the system" it could itself advocate. Thereby it acquired enough flexibility to adapt the competitive social order to certain revolutionary interests of the working class and even of the indigent sectors. Nevertheless, even if this advance did not come about, the conflict of values and interests did not necessarily by itself engender confusion between the two kinds of pressure, so that the "pressures within the system" from the lower classes or the ultra-radical bourgeois strata were stigmatized and outlawed by repressive means, simply because of the propagation of "pressures against the system." Finally, although the bourgeois ruling strata regularly took advantage of class tensions and conflicts, they rarely saw themselves called upon to use the "pressures within the system" and the "pressures against the system" of the working class, or the destitute masses, as a standard device to fortify their own privileges over other bourgeois sectors or as a systematic means for obtaining sporadic advantages. Class behavior so elementary and crude might have been necessary in times when the class regime was in crisis or when the pattern of bourgeois hegemony was undergoing changes, during electoral campaigns, or in "common fronts" for or against certain government policies, etc. Nevertheless, the degree of vertical differentiation and horizontal integration of the bourgeois classes established bourgeois rule and bourgeois power on firmer, more flexible, and more stable political and material foundations. As a general consequence, the pattern of social reaction to "pressures from below" in favor of or against the existing order was normally more tolerant, flexible, and democratic. Thus certain values of bourgeois democracy established themselves side by side with the material, legal, and political requisites for the actual existence, continuation, and consolidation of bourgeois domination and power. As a result, bourgeois consensus was able to "open up" the existing order to these pressures as part of a routine that conferred on the citizenry, on the political freedoms provided by the legal system, on the political participation of the masses, etc., the attribute of being something essential for the stability and normality of a national society.

Dependent and underdeveloped class society has a variegated history, with a variety of forces operating. To take the example of Brazil, in the course of this past half-century the bourgeois classes and their substrata found themselves face to face with pressures both favorable and contrary to the established social order: some originated within bourgeois sectors or at least were manipulated by them, others were of a specifically working-class origin or were of a "popular" stamp. The picture was the inverse of what we have just described. "Pressures within the system," often spurred or radicalized by the intermediate sectors and even by the urban high bourgeoisie, developed in a negative historical climate. The vertical differentiation and horizontal integration of the bourgeois classes and their substrata was not sufficient nor complex enough to engender any sort of average bourgeois consensus of the democratic type. Indeed bourgeois radicalism, in taking these external forms, was more the expression of a historical impatience than a structural process of radicalization of dissatisfied and rebellious sectors of the bourgeoisie. In terms of the composition of the bourgeoisie and its relation with the organization of national society, there was no coherent and socially necessary tendency of consistent and militant bourgeois radicalism. In the light of this situation, the bourgeoisie had no way to resolve the antagonistic or semi-divergent interests of the other classes, despite the fact that those interests derived from the very structure and dynamics of the existing social order. Bourgeois radicalism was not able to grow in that direction, simultaneously dynamizing bourgeois rule and bourgeois power. The "pressures within the system" fomented by the working classes or the masses, with or without the backing of extremist sectors of the bourgeoisie, were popping up everywhere, threatening to become a veritable historical deluge. However, bourgeois consensus proved invariably timid and hostile to these pressures. Indeed it had every cause to fear them, given the distribution of wealth and power in a dependent and underdeveloped class society. The mass of those who ranked themselves within the system was too small to render the bourgeois condition an element of economic, social, and political stability, while very many did not consider themselves part of the system, or only marginally or partially so. This has stirred up class fears and made social unrest something to be dreaded. As a result, society's reaction to the pressures within the system reflected a very specifically bourgeois political mentality —inflexible, and intolerant even of symbolic and compensatory manifestations of bourgeois radicalism and moreover, ready to obstruct or prevent their advance, in particular their potential for accelerating the national revolution.

This kind of social reaction was directly rooted in an extremely vulnerable form of class fear. It was not the product of intellectual or political obscurantism. There had never been any question about what the pressures within the system would represent in either ideal terms (for the existence of a democratic regime) or concrete terms (to get the "Brazilian revolution" out of its deadlock). Nonetheless, that pattern of social reaction carried inflexibility and intolerance very far, as if it had been systematically obscurantist and immovable. The "pressures within the system" were likened to "pressures against the system" as a practical expedient to facilitate the stigmatization of the former and to improve, *en bloc*, the efficacy of the system of oppression and repression, which thus permitted the conservative sectors of the bourgeoisie to monopolize the choice of historically necessary innovations. Given this context, "enlightened" bourgeois radicalism was easily equated with "subversion" and "communism," while the "pressures against the system" were in general stripped of any moral, legal, or political legitimacy. However, it was not a question of historical immobility or an obstinate defense of stagnation. On the contrary, the bourgeois strata were just as open to changes in the system from within as to "modernization steered from without," *provided that the*

conditions and the effects of such processes were under conserva-
tive control. The important point is that the bourgeois classes and
their substrata were not only incapable of getting out of their own
skin, but the way in which the Brazilian version of class society
functioned and grew prevented the bourgeoisie, as long as existing
conditions persisted, from establishing any flexible response to
pressures within the system stemming from the working and destitute classes, or from absorbing pressures against the system stemming from the same groups. Bourgeois rule and bourgeois power
therefore remained narrowly restricted to the interests and instru-
mentalities of the bourgeois classes. Bourgeois consensus was unable to expand with the direct and indirect support of the other
classes, which were not linked up with the bourgeoisie either
through egalitarian impulses of national integration or through the
material dynamics of economic participation or the social dynamics
of political and cultural participation. By closing themselves off,
the bourgeois classes and their substrata narrowed their historical
field of action and their creative political maneuvering room,
whether reformist or revolutionary.

Thus what we have is not the "ideal" competitive social order,
but that which proved possible in a dependent and underdeveloped
class society. It fitted dependent capitalism, uneven internal development, and external imperialist domination like a glove, although it does not even remotely resemble the flexibility of this
order under conditions of an autonomous or hegemonic capitalist
development. Nor has it been able to fulfill its "normal functions"
of dynamizing the class regime. This is because it is a competitive
social order in which only those who qualify are admitted to the
competition, those who are propertied, rich, and powerful. What is
worse, at the historical level this competitive social order persists
and is altered only through the connection of the domination and
power of the possessing classes with the neutralization or exclusion of the other classes, who are either disqualified, and therefore
remain inactive, or are allowed to compete, but not freely, and
therefore remain its wards. Nonetheless, this sequence of relationships binds lord and slave together in such a way that the fate of
the former is dependent on the latter. Even to acquire more historical freedom or more political maneuvering room, the bourgeois
classes and substrata, in their capacity as bourgeoisie, had to go
beyond their frontiers to seek material and political support and in
the last instance transfer the deepest dynamic forces of the compe-

titive social order to the laboring classes and the excluded groups of the society. This is not merely the basis of a "populist demagogy." In it is also to be found the essence of the Brazilian Republican regime, with its authoritarian presidentialism, and it has constituted the fulcrum of the "equilibrium of the system" throughout the entire evolution of class society. Joaquim Nabuco's well-known ideas with regard to the "abolitionist mandate" are perfectly applicable to a citizenship that is affirmed for a few yet is denied to the many: the effective citizen is an "*ex officio* advocate" of the "People" who, however, betrays his mandate and turns it exclusively to his own advantage. In this way the contradictions inherent in class society entered into bourgeois life, suffusing it to the core, and vitiating relations among the bourgeois classes themselves. Despite all its wealth, security, and stability, the bourgeois world shifted the center of its equilibrium to the infernal core of an extremely unjust and inhumane class society whose birth looked like the end of everything. This sociohistorical, psychological, and political situation impoverished and limited bourgeois consensus, which would withdraw into its shell when confronted with concrete historical challenges. It relied solely on "pressures from the top down" which could be mobilized through bourgeois domination or imposed by bourgeois power. Further, in cases of extreme tension, it in fact only believed in pressures that were embodied in and guaranteed by the means of oppression and repression, both ordinary and extraordinary, of the national state.

This brief sociological digression has brought out a crucial point: the crisis of bourgeois power did not coincide with any fundamental movement of the bourgeois classes and their substrata toward the "consolidation" (or "restoration" as it is called by others who take the crisis of the First Republic seriously) of bourgeois democracy in Brazil. On the contrary, it brought these classes and strata face to face with the three focal points of direct and indirect pressures mentioned above, without their having any genuinely coherent collective inclination toward a democratization of class relations. The very structure, and the short-term tendencies toward differentiation within the existing competitive social order could not tolerate such inclinations, which were at variance with the urgent need of investing bourgeois rule and power with a clear-cut pattern of class hegemony. Thus the pressures did not force the bourgeois classes and their substrata to face the problem of democracy (even in the sense of a bourgeois democracy), although they did very much have to contend with the problem of order (that is, a "bourgeois order" which "had to be saved," placed on stable foundations, and "consolidated").

To translate these concepts into clearer terms, the confrontation of the Brazilian bourgeoisie with its structural and historical reality obliged it to take up the dilemma of how to institute openly a collective oligarchy of the propertied classes. Thus the question of autocracy arose, though disguised by the meretricious countenance of a "strong democracy." Only in this way was it able to restrain the incipient or postponed processes of "disaggregation of the system," and move from a "feeble" to a "firm" bourgeois order. Thus the political element was the underpinning of the economic and social, since the resolution of the dilemma entailed inevitable political transformations that went beyond, and opposed, institutionally established patterns of organization of the economy, the society, and the state. The "outward appearances of the system" had to be demolished so that bourgeois domination and power could assume its true identity, enshrining itself in absolute control of the relations of production, the corresponding superstructures, and the ideological apparatus.

Nevertheless, a bourgeoisie economically, socially, and politically impotent to resolve pressures and tensions "within the system" has of course limited historical alternatives. If the real basis of bourgeois power had indeed been solid and flexible, it could have risked making use of bourgeois radicalism and even of "the pressures against the system" to surmount the elementary contradictions facing it and at the same time to widen and broaden the links between its interests and the laboring and destitute classes. This would not have been impossible given the intense (albeit false) climate of reformist nationalism generated by bourgeois radicalism and populist "demagogy." However, these contradictions were "structural" in the sense that they were part of a broader constellation of changes essential to the functioning of a class society and its corresponding competitive social order. To absorb them, the classes would have had to transcend a set of interests shaped by dependency and by unequal internal development. This was the leap which in fact the upper and middle strata of the bourgeoisie were afraid to make, as they demonstrated clearly when put to the test. With their backs to the wall, at critical moments of collective decision, the bourgeois classes definitely rejected any "alliance among the classes," since any accommodation would have brought about an open break with these two poles of capitalist relations and capitalist accumulation. Once the choice was made, it was irreversible, and accelerated, with or without subsequent bourgeois confirmation, a series of deepgoing transformations in the economy, society, and state—a kind of revolution "within the system." The only thing left to do was to get tougher and make organized use of class violence "while there was still time." In this gamble, the class had to impose itself on the nation and prevail over it.

Nevertheless, this path was more difficult than risky. The obstacles lay in the capacity of the bourgeois classes and their substrata for collective action. On the one hand, the degree of vertical differentiation and horizontal integration of these classes fell short of the "historical requirements." Whatever solidarity the bourgeois classes and their substrata had managed to forge was not balanced enough to bring them together in a collective defense of their differences and to dynamize or deepen these differences. In a structural sense, a unifying movement of the bourgeoisie could only be based on that which they had in common, i.e., their status as propertied classes, since the points of difference only drove the bourgeois classes and their substrata into mutual conflict at both the general level of projects of participation in the existing competitive order and at the particular level of the struggle for social control of class power and of the state. On the other hand, the pattern of linkage among the bourgeois classes and their substrata, the product of the economic, social, and political dynamics of the existing competitive order, further aggravated the internal contradictions among the bourgeoisie. The surges of industrial and economic growth made these classes and their substrata, both archaic and modern, susceptible to an intense and uncontrollable greed for new "opportunities" and "strategic advantages." In situations of this sort, the institutions that organize and regulate the behavior and mentality of the bourgeoisie—firms, trade associations, political parties, the state, etc.—did not develop, nor could they, coercive controls of a purgative sort. The "golden rule" prevailed: What was good for the individual was good for the bourgeoisie as a whole, the practical corollary of this being: It is better to experience the negative effects of centrifugal tendencies, which are thereby strengthened, than to struggle against them directly and subject them to deliberate control which is likely to have limited effect. These two attitudes together created a major barrier to any necessary political transformation, immobilizing the ability of the bourgeoisie to act collectively at the level of both class and nation.

None of this is new, and the Brazilian bourgeoisie is neither the first nor the last obliged to confront this "juvenile dilemma." Still the bourgeois classes and their substrata had to confront this dilemma during a period when bourgeois power was experiencing a structural and historical crisis. They did not have time to wait for their own increasing vertical differentiation, horizontal integration, and articulation to promote—after perhaps a quarter of a century, considering the pace at which things were moving—the maturation of the competitive social order, thereby producing a more complex and flexible pattern of class solidarity. Circumstances caused the common class interests to work upon, politically and psychologically, the frustrations and anger inherent in an impasse of this magnitude, rapidly driving the bourgeoisie's class fears to a fever pitch. There arose directly within the heart of the high and middle bourgeoisies, in the institutions that organized and applied bourgeois power, various movements, all ultimately directed toward a contrived and deliberate outcome that would embody the bourgeois will. The objective rather quickly became clear. The best descriptions show that this transformation, which was still in a rudimentary and inchoate phase during the Estado Novo, reached its peak among the conservative forces that galvanized the candidacy of Janio Quadros for the presidency, bringing into focus the political manipulation of what may be called for want of a better expression the "tactical unity" of the bourgeois classes and their various substrata. Powerless to resolve their differences, they shifted the focus for unity of action away from the grand historical options and toward the collective self-defense of their common material interests as propertied classes. Consequently, we may describe the resultant pattern of bourgeois hegemony as an aggregate hegemony, a mere mechanical adhering together of class interests. The qualification, however, is not meant derisively; on the contrary, no sociologist can be unaware of what such a transformation implies both structurally and politically. It amounted literally to a bourgeois "acceleration of history." Without substantially changing themselves, the nation, or their material relations with the other classes, the bourgeois classes and their substrata discovered an equivalent to the structural and dynamic conditions of class domination that had not been within their reach. Even before bringing the entire complex process of vertical differentiation, horizontal integration, and articulation to completion, they managed by political means to establish a kind of unification that would enable them to achieve the same ends, at least as long as bourgeois power was unforeseeably eroding and supposedly in mortal danger. Elementary and crude though it may have been, this form of bourgeois hegemony placed the control of time, space, and society in the hands of the bourgeoisie, thereby setting the internal rhythms of intensive industrialization and the development of monopoly capitalism under the existing competitive social order.

Since it did not reflect prior structural changes of the internal social environment, the consolidation of an aggregate or articulated pattern of bourgeois hegemony may seem to be a phenomenon of no importance, superficial and secondary to a conventional sociological analysis. Nevertheless, its mere possibility, the fact that the bourgeois classes sought to realize it historically, would itself effect a significant change in the Brazilian class system. Once this pattern of hegemony became established, altering abruptly in the aftermath the scope of bourgeois domination and the efficacy of bourgeois power, its precise sociological significance became clear. A fundamental qualitative change had taken place in the sociodynamic and political potential of bourgeois class domination and power. Though the ensuing transformation may have been insufficient to modify the structures and dynamics of the class system as a whole, it did permit the bourgeoisie to reduce and bypass the political, sociocultural, and economic obstacles before it, and in this way to overcome, temporarily at least, its historical impotence. It is this aspect, we think, which must be kept in mind, and emphasized in a sociological analysis. The qualitative change in the political, sociocultural, and economic forces that had become concentrated in the hands of the bourgeois classes and their substrata conferred upon them a new historical opportunity, as if previous structural changes in the "internal social environment" had taken place, in the bourgeoisie's favor, and as if bourgeois power had not suffered from such severe inherent defects. The unification of class interests and class solidarity, rooted in those elements of the material situation that were shared universally, although to an unequal degree, by all sectors of the bourgeoisie as the propertied classes, served, as mentioned, the function of concentrating and centralizing socially the economic, sociocultural, and political forces over which they disposed. In this way the bourgeois classes and their substrata could take advantage both structurally and dynamically of "their small numbers," which they did in a conscious, deliberate, and organized manner. This centralization of real power took place simultaneously at two levels—that of direct class relations and that of class domination as mediated by the national state. Thus the two congenital defects that undermined bourgeois power, rendering it incapable of countering the centrifugal tendencies that were rending it asunder and reducing it politically to zero, compensated one another. Since it was the material interests common to all the sectors of the bourgeoisie, as the propertied classes, that prevailed in these processes, and since the shift of real power was consequently toward the static nucleus of the existing competitive social order, the unification and centralization of bourgeois power went far enough to resist the direct reactive effects, inescapably disintegrative, of their conversion into "historical factors." The bourgeoisie as a whole was at least able to bring about, in a matter of one or two decades or a quarter of a century—the period during which its most conservative tendencies were able to hold sway on the historical scene—the abundant modernization consequent to intensive industrialization and the emergence of monopoly capitalism. In a word, it became free to give bourgeois self-affirmation the character of a counter-revolution, which meant that the rush of modernization was to be inevitably associated with a moral regeneration and the stability of the system.

However, this evolution depended on something more than a mere change in "bourgeois will" and in the way the collective behavior of the dominant strata of the bourgeois classes was organized. As we have pointed out, the transformation in question here was a general response to the pressures of bourgeois radicalism, workers' opposition, and popular dissatisfaction. The unification and centralization of the real power of the bourgeois classes and various substrata—at the level of direct class relations and mediation by the national state—had, if they were to be politically "useful" and "efficient," to go beyond the narrow limits of the bourgeois classes and the very real physical frontiers of bourgeois domination. That is, the dominant strata of the bourgeois classes lacked that excess quantum of power that might have enabled them to dispel pro-bourgeois nonconformist pressures and antibourgeois pressures, and to guarantee themselves a maximum of historical autonomy in the class control of the series of transformations subsequently undergone by the system. Thus, unmistakably, the self-defense of the bourgeoisie was organized and armed as a historic movement of self-assertion and of the assertion of the privileges of bourgeois class interests. This was not a passive self-defense, but active, militant, and aggressive, and within the historical limitations of dependent capitalism it assumed a triumphant historical dimension. This delimits the nature of the two processes of unification and centralization of real class power. At the level of direct class relations, and at the level of the national state in its mediating role, the bourgeois classes and their substrata defended the monopoly of a "sound citizenry," and accordingly reaped the political dividends of this bourgeois control of civil society and of the national state itself. Even before they became conspiratorial and burst forth as a counter-revolution in defense of dependent modernization and the regeneration of morality and order, the two processes were pointing in this direction. Hence the extensive and intensive class mobilization of all the material, ideological, political, and armed resources within its reach that has characterized the collective self-defense of the Brazilian bourgeoisie since 1945.

From this standpoint, the bourgeois minority was able to draw on a broad structural base to establish and exploit politically this self-defensive consensus. The bourgeois classes and their substrata extended themselves throughout all levels of organization of civil society and the national state. On them the normality and continuity could depend as readily as the crisis and collapse of both. They might neutralize all functions that were more or less fundamental for the survival of the existing social order, or they might seize control of the situation and distort these functions in whatever way became advisable. The radical sectors of the petty, middle, and high bourgeoisie, together with the mobilized sectors of the working classes and the impoverished classes, were able to do little or nothing to obstruct this state of affairs. Bourgeois "sabotage" of the system meant literally the sabotage of the existing order as such. This became apparent as the sabotaging effect of bourgeois initiatives began to undermine the precarious representative regime; it became obvious after the counter-revolutionary coup, when autocratic bourgeois purges and controls were instituted. In the light of the essential evidence it seems clear that the processes of unification and centralization of bourgeois power rested on a quite broad structural foundation and that this base was mobilized in breadth and depth; these elements are key to explaining the sudden emergence and at the same time the success of the counter-revolution. The latter was not hatched from these two processes like a chicken from an egg. These processes of unification and centralization, however, forged the transformation that led to counter-revolution as a logical culmination: they established the link between the modernizing upsurge and the regeneration of morality and order, and turned, by unusual means, the class self-defense of the bourgeoisie into self-assertion and the acquisition of class privilege.

It is debatable whether this linkage could have been avoided by the conflicting historical forces and, more particularly, whether the bourgeoisie's self-defensive reaction need have been so pervasively and unyieldingly military and technocratic. Neither point has more than academic importance. The facts themselves demonstrate concretely to what degree these events were inexorable. Still, it is important at least to take these two points into consideration since they are helpful in pinpointing the key aspects of the autocratic bourgeois conservative reaction.

As for the first point, the "collapse of populism" was essentially a collapse of bourgeois radicalism and of the pseudo-democratic bourgeois order that had engendered it. The lack of solid political links, which might have been both flexible and strong, between the propertied classes and the working and destitute classes sapped the existing competitive social order of any effective and irreversible democratic potential. "Populist demagogy" did not derive from any real pluralism—it was an openly tolerated manipulation of the masses. The "People" had neither responsible spokesmen nor loyal advocates in the "bourgeois camp"; and when the democratic game became too risky, the actors took off their masks. In a word, bourgeois democracy was not *weak*, but *disguised*. This may seem to be an excessively harsh description. But what other may be painted after all that has happened and is still going on? Nor were the masses derelict. There was no "moment of historical default" by the masses. What did occur, as the analysts of populism have clearly shown, was a "moment of attempted affirmation" by the masses, or a tacit accord on a "new social pact," as some authors would have it, suppressed in an unprecedented manner by the bourgeoisie's reactive self-defense. Thus, the link could have been bypassed *if* history had been otherwise. But since history was not otherwise, it clearly defined what the bourgeois classes and their substrata were aiming at in abolishing the democratic bourgeois appearances of the established order.

As for the second point, it is obvious that the pervasiveness of the military and the technocrats was but a product, albeit an essential one. The bourgeois classes and their substrata could have dispensed with this penetration only if they had been able to rely on a broad structural support from the working and destitute classes. In this case, however, it would have been absurd for them to undertake a modernizing and rejuvenating counter-revolution. The stigmatizing of bourgeois radicalism would have served no purpose, since the competitive social order would have been open to all the pressures, conformist as well as nonconformist, falling within the orbit of "democratic pluralism." The hard facts, however, reveal the contrary, namely that the self-defensive reaction of the bourgeoisie was only able to mature with a strong and continuing military and the technocratic presence. It followed from the aggregated pattern of bourgeois hegemony that the key tasks of the counter-revolutionary, self-defensive historical movement would be transferred to certain civil, and mainly military sectors of the bourgeoisie. It is quite certain that if the middle and upper strata of the Brazilian bourgeoisie had not been firmly and massively entrenched within the state, forming a true bureaucratic bourgeoisie invested with state power and a broad freedom to use it, the unification and centralization of bourgeois power would have evolved in a historical vacuum. Instead of culminating with a counter-revolution and the restoration of the bourgeois order, they would have resulted in an aggravation of the conflicts with "the number one enemy" and would perhaps have crumbled miserably. In this respect, the penetration by the military and the technocrats of the various phases of the movement—conspiracy, offensive, consolidation of power, etc.—as well as of the autocratic-bourgeois "regenerated" national state, was an intrinsic part of the self-defensive reaction of the bourgeoisie and was instrumental for the immanent historical ends of its self-assertion and self-bestowal of privileges. If neither had occurred, and even more, if neither had achieved such high and persistent levels, the crisis of bourgeois power would probably have culminated in a revolution "against the system." Even if such a revolution had been initiated on the strength of bourgeois radicalism and had persisted for a certain time under the control of this radicalism, it is unlikely that it could have been contained within this limit and entrenched itself in a democratic-bourgeois order sufficiently strong to absorb the anti-bourgeois pressures of the working and destitute classes and the revolutionary socialist movement.

There remains the question of the duration and intensity of this pervasion of the structures and functions of the national state by the military and the technocrats. Some think that a power external to the bourgeoisie, or indeed, the bourgeois consensus itself, may turn against this process. While such a question lies beyond the present discussion, we may still air it briefly in passing. A power external to the bourgeoisie has not put in its appearance as a historical alternative; if and when it does emerge it will have to do so on the basis of the existing national state, organizing itself into a ruling class and carrying out its own revolution. For this class therefore, the relationship with the forces responsible for the penetration of the state by the military and the technocrats will depend on concrete situations which cannot be determined in advance. What matters now is the concrete alternative that in fact has taken shape and is becoming history: bourgeois consensus, about which only dour observations can be made. This is a consensus linked to the autocratic tendencies of the Brazilian bourgeoisie by virtue of the structure of class society and of the counter-revolutionary cast assumed by the bourgeois self-defensive reaction. Not only does the bourgeois consensus welcome militarization and technocratization as processes serving to consolidate the established order; it would only stand to lose if it did the contrary. Bourgeois consensus itself reflects this polarization, having become the sole source of legitimation of the two processes and their consequences. It is only the "first-class" citizens of the civil society who sanction these processes and ardently defend their "necessity" and "legitimacy." But again, things could not have been otherwise. This legitimation is merely the abstract and ideal expression of what bourgeois consensus is about at the practical level. Without this intense and continuing militarization and technocratization, it would be impossible to put the national state at the center of the historical transformations in progress, and, accordingly, it would also be impossible to maintain the link between modernization and the regeneration of morality and the established order and to transform the reactive self-defense of an "embattled bourgeoisie" into a source of bourgeois self-assertion and self-bestowal of privilege. Thus bourgeois consensus is but the translation of bourgeois rationality into pragmatic and realistic terms.

The three processes discussed above reflect the broad historical transformations that have been taking place in the organization of bourgeois power and of class society in the last half of this century. The unification and centralization of the class power of the bourgeoisie show how solidarity among the bourgeois classes and their substrata were altered and how a new composite pattern of hegemony of these classes and substrata emerged, spread, and was entrenched. In turn, the bourgeois counter-revolution illustrates the passage from the economic and the social to the political: how the bourgeois classes and their substrata imposed their own economic, social, and political transformation on the other classes, bringing about profound changes in the institutional patterns of class relations, the organization of the national state, and the links between bourgeois class interests and the economic, social, and political rhythms of integration of the nation as a whole. Historically, the change was purely and simply from a disguised and paternalistic bourgeois class dictatorship to an open and rigid one. It was a shift that outwardly appeared to be irrelevant, especially to outside observers accustomed to the idea that "they know that they are doing," "that's the only way some countries can be governed." Nonetheless, a reality so uncompromisingly terrible and shattering may still be getting better or getting worse. Those who have to shoulder the economic, social, and political costs of this transformation may find themselves in an even more acute state of relative privation and systematic oppression, revealing whether the change took place for the benefit of some and the loss of others. Since the economy, the society, and the state were all equally involved in this transformation, there was no area or domain in which the negative, transitory, or lasting consequences were not reflected—lowering wages and job security, restricting the right to strike and the right of working-class protest; lowering the educational aspirations of the "lower" classes and reducing opportunities for democratic education; restricting civil and political rights; imposing political and police-military constraints, etc.

The terms "reduce" and "restrict" express quite well the substance of the relation of the new civil society constituted by "first-class" citizens, almost all bourgeois, to the national state and the nation. The static and dynamic equilibrium of the rigid and undisguised class dictatorship ideally required the stripping away of reactive controls and the reactive power of self-defense or retaliation by either the dominated classes in general or the dissident sectors of the ruling classes. While, on the one hand, by their very nature these three processes deepened the intermeshing of bourgeois power with the national state, on the other, the establishment and maintenance of an undisguised and rigid class dictatorship transformed the national state into a nucleus of bourgeois power and into the fulcrum of the historical events that marked the evolution of the bourgeoisie from self-defense to self-affirmation and the self-bestowal of privileges. For better or for worse, therefore, it was through the national state that this class dictatorship would show the political parameters of the autocratic bourgeois model of capitalist transformation.

If the other conditions are maintained or undergo but minor change, the acceleration of the bourgeois revolution—the historical fruit of intensive industrialization and the development of monopoly capitalism—must lead to a growth and aggravation of the already existing social, political, and economic inequalities. It is easy to observe how this took place concretely. It is more difficult, however, to draw pertinent political conclusions from such observations.

In the first place, this relationship between the acceleration of the bourgeois revolution and the distribution of wealth, social prestige, and power in a class society presupposes that the economic, sociocultural, and political distance between civil society and the nation does not diminish but increases beyond measure in all directions as the acceleration proceeds. The hardening of the system is automatic and preliminary in such a situation: the national state must assume new functions, differentiate the old functions or carry them out with greater rigor, which means an intensification of direct and indirect repression, inherent to "system maintenance." In the context of events, the self-defense of the bourgeoisie, as a product of a counter-revolutionary bourgeois movement, included the possible recourse to civil war, which, however, did not come about because of the lack of response, and also because the coup d'état proved to be a sufficient means for effecting the political transition. The hardening of the system followed a natural path toward an excessive and unnecessary display of "preventive" force. This linked the militarization of the state's repressive functions and the safeguarding of national security to the creation of a new *status quo* necessary for the establishment and maintenance of an undisguised and rigid class dictatorship. In the short run, it was the task of the national state to "depress" and "compress" the political and legal space of all classes and substrata, even bourgeois and pro-bourgeois, that opposed the transition by violent or peaceful means. Over the long term, their task was more complex, namely, to create the legal framework of a competitive social order that would possess special regulatory mechanisms against "revolutionary war," political "agitation," and the "subversive manipulation" of discontent. The institutionalization of violence was not the most remarkable element of the process (that was already present in the oppressive and repressive arsenal of the national state), but rather the scope and character of the functions that tied the national state and the militarization of many of its services and structures to a conception of security as the *permanent war* of one class against the other. Unlike a disguised and paternalistic class dictatorship, the new class dictatorship admitted of no ambiguities. Although dissimulation still had a role, since things could not be spelled out clearly and reality could not be depicted as it was, it would have been impossible to avoid a clear definition of the class enemies and the real or potential situations of class conflict without seriously impairing the effectiveness of the "state security organs." On the other hand, a militant and aggressive philosophy of defense of the established order entails rather rigorous correlation between "crime" and "punishment." Many see this as the level of military and police action, but it is legal and political as well, and there bourgeois autocracy erected its ideal of a state historically descended from Fascism and Nazism. It is not the essential function of the state to safeguard the network of political relations among unequal classes. Its principal function is to eliminate any need for a spontaneous political network, since the state itself prescribes without appeal the order which must prevail and which must be respected.

In the second place, it was necessary that the essential political controls over economic life be diverted from the nation and, by both visible and invisible means, gathered into the hands of civil society. The question is not, as many think, merely the simple and direct means used by the bourgeois classes to protect themselves from the reactions of the working and destitute classes against growing economic inequalities, or more generally against the brutal increase of their "economic burden." Beyond all this, there was the need to revolutionize the means of capital accumulation imposed by intensive industrialization and by the development of monopoly capitalism. On the whole, therefore, the economic exigencies of the situation tend to transform bourgeois consensus, established and defined on the basis of civil society, into an equivalent substitute for a national consensus. These exigencies, among other things, required the continuation of the counter-revolution and through it, an economic stranglehold on the system. Earlier, we considered the economic significance of the political shift. Now it remains only to pinpoint the concrete form that this shift took and what it signified for the political linkage of the competitive social order in a state of counter-revolutionary tension.

Two devices made it possible to transpose bourgeois consensus from civil society to the nation. First, the military and technocratic penetration of the services, structures, and functions of the state increased the size of the bureaucratic bourgeoisie and broadened its direct participation in the conduct of the affairs of state. Further, it resulted in more specific, flexible, and efficient controls over the functioning and transformation of the state by the ruling strata of the bourgeois classes. Second, the political links among the ruling strata of the bourgeois classes and between them and the state were modernized. Bourgeois interests thus overcame their congenital political debility. They no longer had to "pressure" the state by indirect and unsure means (parliament, the mass media, manipulation of strikes and popular unrest, etc.), and instead carried out the necessary adjustments in ways that were less visible externally but were better adapted to the technical and political requirements of speed, firmness, efficiency, security, economy, etc. As regards the meaning of the political shift, two distinct maneuvers are evident. (1) During the stages of the bourgeois revolution the economic revolution was separated from the national revolution, which was relegated to the secondary plane. (2) The dependent capitalist state during its modernization was transformed into a link of the economic stage of the bourgeois revolution, which led it systematically to neglect those of its economic functions which were connected to the national revolution or its acceleration. The bourgeois classes and their substrata have therefore always favored a *sui generis* state interventionism. Controlled in the last instance by private initiative, at one extreme this interventionism inclines toward a state-directed capitalism and at the other toward an authoritarian state. The two conceptions are ambiguous, but they do reflect a concrete reality. The state assumes capitalist structures and functions and through them moves forward over the terrain of political despotism, not so as to serve real national interests flowing from the intensification of the national revolution but to satisfy the bourgeois consensus, of which it has become the instrument, and to give historical viability to an extremist ideology of development, the true infantile disorder of monopoly capitalism at the periphery.

Third, the described relationship requires that civil society be able to assume control of the political life of the nation. This was not a question of a collective urge that shifted national consensus to bourgeois consensus. That would have been unrealizable, since the concentration of legal and political power was not materialized in the same way as the concentration of economic power and wealth. Furthermore, the legal and political order of a class society, to have validity and instrumental utility (even for the bourgeois classes or the ruling bourgeois strata), must be universal. Therefore in the juridical and political sphere it was impossible to superimpose bourgeois consensus upon national consensus and cause it to prevail over the latter without risks of a regressive breakdown of the legal and political order. To prevail, even through a legally and politically counter-revolutionary movement, civil society was obliged to rely upon its social monopoly over legal and political power, and at the same time to impose its will on the nation from within the legal and political order as though it were itself the objective manifestation of this order, its ideal and corporeal embodiment. This process unfolded in several stages, which we cannot pursue further in the present discussion. It behooves us to point out merely that it created certain requirements for the self-defense of the bourgeois classes which were different before and after the institution of the undisguised and rigid class dictatorship, and that the structural and dynamic requirements of bourgeois rule changed once that happened. Those who think in terms of the repression of workers, student strikes, and popular protest, the destruction of the foundations of the nationalist-reformist and socialist movements or the undermining of the "revolutionary war," will see but one phase of the process and one part of the overall social picture. There is another side, which emerged in the course of successive dramatic events of the "secure" and "constructive" phases of the counter-revolution, experienced by the bourgeois classes in their campaign of self-affirmation and self-bestowed privilege. During these phases, alongside the repressive and destructive controls which have remained, a deeper and broader effort appeared, aimed at rendering the counter-revolution effective, entrenching bourgeois rule, and broadening bourgeois power. This meant the creation and application of new juridical and political structures, and the modernization of existing ones, the renovation and rationalization of the state machinery of oppression and repression, and the adaptation of the entire ideological and utopian apparatus of the bourgeoisie to a counter-revolutionary situation which had "come to stay."

Thus we see that bourgeois consensus reconciled the Brazilian tradition of limited democracy—democracy among equals, i.e., among the powerful, who dominate and represent civil society—with the "modernizing trend" of strong government. The legal and political order is kept "open," "democratic," and "universal," maintaining the values that enshrine the state based on law. The state, in turn, materializes historically to the extent that all this is necessary for the monopolization of real power, authority, and control of the sources of legitimacy by the bourgeois classes and their elites. The formal or positive validity of the legal and political order, however, is distinct from actual workings: in practice, civil laws and political guarantees are effectuated in accordance with extra-judiciary and extra-political criteria. The counter-revolution did not create this historical situation: it inherited it from the Old Republic and the Empire. But it has distinguished itself by its intransigent defense of the inherited *status quo* and by its autocratic conception of the "stability of the system," which is not seen in terms of a confluence of the two determining factors in question but in the light of an ideal parallelism which specifies that "everything must remain in its place." In a word, democracy, as the human praxis of an entire nation, could only be achieved at some infinite point in the future, where these two parallel lines would meet. It is not just that democracy is dissociated from bourgeois self-affirmation; it was also a tremendous obstacle to the kind of self-bestowal of privilege which the bourgeois classes required, to be able to confront intensive industrialization and the transition to monopoly capitalism.

It is important to stress that the legal and political order was obliged not only to favor the appropriation of privilege by the bourgeois classes, who provide the civil society's "first-class" citizens. At the same time it was also pressured (albeit not in proportion or steadily) to curb dissident and other classes by compressing or eliminating their political space.

The innovations and modernization introduced by the counter-revolution into juridical and political relations aimed at adapting the order to the requirement that the two processes be simultaneous and interdependent. The undisguised and rigid class dictatorship, therefore, attempted to turn the undermining of the system into a perennial process at the same time that it created for that process a context of systematic and permanent political pressure. It has not rejected the formal practices of bourgeois democracy; on the contrary, it has continually recurred to them in its utopian call for a "return to normality." It has, however, required, both objectively and ideally, a neo-absolutist emergency state, of aristocratic or elitist inspiration and in essence oligarchic, which could unite the self-legitimating revolutionary will of the bourgeoisie with a pragmatic republican legalism and a class despotism of a military and technocratic stamp. This is the price to be paid for the pseudo-"reconciliation." To overcome the contradiction inherent in this duality of the order (the undermining process has actually given rise to two superimposed orders, one legal and "ideal," the other real and "possible"), the national state has developed into a political colossus. On the one hand it has become the source of a sacrosanct and indisputable authority, and on the other the center of an absolute and total power. This, however, was the only way that such a state could transcend its congenital weakness, establishing the basis of its own political unity and the political integration of the nation during or beyond the two simultaneous but mutually exclusive moments of self-affirmation of civil society and negation of the national community.

This discussion shows that these three processes (the unification and the centralization of bourgeois class power, and the bourgeois counter-revolution) were leading to the typical model of the modern capitalist state, in the form it assumes at the periphery, when dependent capitalism and the corresponding class society have reached the phase of intensive industrialization and the transition to monopoly capitalism. The form is that of a complex and heterogeneous national state containing various historical levels, as if in it were reflected the extremes, the point of departure and the point of arrival, of all the transformations through which the capitalist state had originally passed in the hegemonic and central society. It combines structures and dynamics—functional and historical—that are contradictory in the extreme but are otherwise in accord with the also extremely contradictory historical situation of the dependent bourgeoisies and class society of dependent capitalism. The basis of this unique complexity is well known and has already been pointed out: the bourgeois classes must affirm and protect themselves, and appropriate privileges through two distinct types of antagonisms—those directed against the working and destitute classes, who are regarded as the principal enemy, and those directed against the bourgeoisies and the sources of power in the hegemonic capitalist societies and the world capitalist system, who were regarded as the principal ally. The contradictions are inherent in the structures and dynamics of class society under dependent capitalism; they undermine bourgeois domination, the real power of the bourgeoisie, class solidarity and bourgeois class hegemony, and the peripheral and dependent capitalist state.[4]

According to our description, the final version of this form of the state, which is becoming entrenched as monopoly capitalism spreads into similarly developing areas of the periphery of the capitalist world, is a syncretic national state. In certain respects it calls to mind the ideal nuclear model, as if it were a representative, democratic, and pluralist state; in other respects it is the consummate expression of a perfect oligarchy, which in its objective outward appearance is as paternalist and traditional as it is authoritarian and modern; finally, certain of its aspects are unmistakably Fascist—coercion, repression, and oppression, and the institutionalization of violence and terror. In describing this state as a "rigid and undisguised class dictatorship" no resemblance to the so-called "traditional political dictatorships" is intended, much less to the more elementary models of political dictatorship imposed through absolute control of the traditional means of force. The state differentiates and saturates its constitutional and functional structure in such a way that it becomes obvious either that it practices routinely a limited democracy or that it negates democracy. It is, literally, an autocratic and oligarchic state. It retains democratic structures and functions, but in behalf of those who monopolize economic, social, and political power and utilize the state to maintain an intrinsic legal and political duality, thanks to which what is oligarchy and oppression for the subject majority is automatically democracy and freedom for the dominant minority. Yet one cannot say that this class dictatorship is transitory and that its political system is destined to fade away as the "threats to the established order" are eliminated. Actually, what is occurring is a process of reorganization of the structures and functions of the national state under the given historical conditions of class relations. The state and the legal and political order are being simultaneously transformed, adapting concomitantly to external and internal conditions invested with a certain continuity. In the end, it would be useless to analyze this state exhaustively. There is no one and only way to understand and describe the dependent and peripheral capitalist state. A product of a situation that is more contradictory and anarchic than any bourgeoisie could survive, it is a syncretic solution and must be accepted as such. One must turn to anthropology to achieve any degree of understanding of this national state. It is otherwise impossible to grasp how an institution can be organized and work despite so many reciprocally corrosive and destructive influences, although they objectify with a certain unity, compatible with their social use. It is Leviathan on one side and Behemoth on the other, but it exists and has some value only because these two aspects complement one another, like the two faces of a coin.[5]

This national state ought not to have emerged at the peak of the bourgeois revolution. Nonetheless, under the conditions of dependent capitalist development it was necessitated by the rhythms of historical, social, and political development that this revolution assumed at the periphery, within Europe and outside of it. The bourgeois revolution was fragmented by a chronically lagging industrialization, detached from the development of the internal market, the agrarian revolution, and the urban revolution, or taking place without those processes' attaining sufficient intensity and making up lost ground only through state intervention and the external push from the dynamic of world capitalism. That which had an impressive degree of synchrony, at least in certain countries of Europe and to a considerable extent in the United States, tends at the periphery to take place in an atomized disjunctive fashion, in more or less discrete stages. As capitalism matures and takes on a modern complexion, the transitions become increasingly more difficult, dangerous, or even cataclysmic. As a consequence, the national state ends up functioning mainly as a compensatory factor, indeed the only one that can be mobilized by the bourgeoisies of the periphery and used compactly to resolve these dilemmas and overcome the organic weakness that gave rise to them. Therefore it is not without reason that the national state has the two faces mentioned above, and that at the extreme it represents such a monstrous mixture of cunning, brute force, and rationality.

In the last instance, it is in this autocratic model of the capitalist state that the "freedom" and the "capacity for rational action" of the dependent bourgeoisie ultimately resides. It provides the bourgeois classes and their substrata with the foundations of bourgeois domination and power, once class society has reached a point critical to its survival. Most important, it gives them the political space they lack to intervene in a deliberate and organized fashion, as a function of their relative potentialities, in the historical course of the bourgeois revolution, slowing down some rhythms, accelerating others, to maintain economic, social, and political processes each at the speed required. Without the absolute control of power which the bourgeois classes derive from the constitution of this state, they could not conceivably succeed in appropriating for themselves with any degree of security the tremendous share of the national economic surplus that accrues to them; nor could they succeed in dissociating, almost at their pleasure, democracy, capitalist development, and national revolution.

It is natural that the disrupting elements of this capitalist state reach their plenitude in the epoch of world confrontation between capitalism and socialism. This confrontation has turned the periphery into one vast battlefield where the dependent capitalist state appears in a wider context, indeed, as a decisive factor in the battle. To defend themselves, to continue to exist and to grow, the dependent national bourgeoisies have no alternative—given the polarization of their situation, of submission to imperialism—other than that we have described. It has situated the bourgeois national and democratic state in a context of organized and institutionalized violence on an international scale, rending it from top to bottom, and turning it into an unrecognizable but efficient political entity. Thus while its modernization has followed the transformations brought about by the evolution of the capitalist state in the hegemonic and central nations, it has not left in its traces any epical inspiration for the realization or emancipation of man within history. Frontiers of this sort are extrinsic and prohibited to this state, except insofar as they are posed in terms of a revolution against the system, which today are of socialist orientation. And if they do come to be formulated by mischance, as happens sometimes with bourgeois radicalism, the confusion is quickly dispelled. This is a truth hard to swallow by those who conceive of the system only from the narrow and exclusive focal point of what is given, the *de facto*, existing reality, as if any alternatives are and would always be determined by conservative thought and conduct.

But if this is not the case, how then can we explain the persever-
ence of the bourgeois classes in their continuing devotion, in Brazil,
to speeding up the economic side of its revolution, submerging
themselves totally in the neurosis of an extremist ideology of development as they stifle with their own hands any possibility of
the classes living together democratically, and of an effective national political community?

Continuation or collapse of the bourgeois autocracy?

The fourth subject we have selected to discuss in this chapter is
the political prospect of this autocratic bourgeois model of capitalist transformation. The preceding discussion endeavored to
show that the composite and complex model of bourgeois hegemony rests on precarious structural and historical underpinnings.
It undoubtedly generated the "surplus of power" that enabled the
bourgeoisie and its elite to unleash open forms of class struggle required by both the transition from competitive to monopoly capitalism and the transition inherent in intensive industrialization. It
was also enabled to set up an autocratic bourgeois capitalist state
which cut off all ties with the past and ultimately established a
new historical point of departure, a dynamic and structural base
for transforming the external unity of the bourgeois classes into an
element in their common political socialization on a national scale.
Nevertheless, the very nature of this autocratic bourgeois state and
the necessity of sustaining with its aid the counter-revolutionary
process which made it possible shows the kind of historical circu-
larity confronted by the bourgeois classes. To overcome this circu-
larity they needed a quite different surplus of power, one that
would provide them not merely an inward class autonomy but also
an outward class autonomy to serve as a foundation to effect a
break with imperialism and thereby provide capitalist development
an autonomous direction.

   If this had been possible, the bourgeois classes and their elites
could have made a typical "revolution within the system" against
external imperialist domination, dependent capitalism, and unequal
internal development. If they were successful, they would have
emerged from the process with a democratic state in their hands
and revolutionary nationalism on their banner. The fact that they
found themselves condemned to permanent counter-revolution in
itself tells another story—*the whole story* that unfolded and is

still unfolding. The unification and centralization of the real power of the bourgeois classes did not reach levels high enough and deep enough—even with the later assistance of its autocratic state and what it represented as a factor reinforcing and stabilizing the system—to alter the significance of the specifically bourgeois interests in terms of the other classes, the nation as a whole, and the centers of external imperialist domination. As a consequence, the bourgeois classes remained imprisoned in their cocoon, isolated from the political reality of a class society, and at the mercy of outside forces as they had been twenty or forty years before. In spite of all, they have alienated themselves from the other classes, the nation, and the Brazilian revolution through that same blind class parochialism that led them to see the working and destitute classes in terms of a narrow alternative: either mere *wards*, or *irreconcilable enemies*. On the other hand, they have no material basis of power for self-affirmation and the appropriation of privileges, except internally, since their famous "authoritarian state" (the euphemism which, revealingly, is used abroad) does not produce the same effects externally, especially in the face of the irrepressible demands of the multinationals, the hegemonic capitalist nations, or their superpower, and the international business community. Thus even the protective functions of the autocratic bourgeois state are inactive or nearly so, since they lack an internal support extending beyond the parochialism of the bourgeois class and putting into the scales the weight of an effectively national countervailing power, backed up by the state. When not a mere smokescreen, any constraints upon the dispositions of the "principal ally" are imposed only in matters where the latter agrees to accept them or to "negotiate."

It appears that the Achilles' heel of bourgeois power lies paradoxically in the factor that accounts for the very possibility of an explosive bourgeois reaction to a situation of apparent or real "historical threat." The composite and segmented bourgeois class solidarity and hegemony made possible a certain unification and centralization, rooted in common interests, but it also restricted bourgeois collective goals and "revolutionary" impulses to the realm of the economic. Two key and parallel limitations emerged. Means and ends, inherently disparate, lost their thrust and effectiveness by being confused and thus transformed artificially—i.e., through a series of compromises, which proceeded more in relation to the "potential risk" than because of a deliberate desire to head off irreme-

diable facts—into collective unities of class political action. Hence
if there was one salient element that suited all, the element that each
stratum of the class would agree upon was absent or present to but
a moderate degree. It is sufficient to consider what they ranked
first: foreign investors, the large Brazilian industrial or commercial
banks, large-scale rural capitalist entrepreneurs, the "traditional"
or "modern" sectors of the middle class, etc. The common element effectively preserved the *status quo* and guaranteed that the
subsequent development of the system would be consonant with
the interests and values of the bourgeoisie, both national and foreign. But it did not serve as the major driving force, which meant
that as far as an acceleration of the bourgeois revolution is concerned it was precisely the variable elements which then became
the most decisive. In addition, the national framework, within
which common bourgeois interests were invested with privilege
and priority status, must be considered. As soon as the bourgeoisie
identified the survival of the system as its principle problem, the
national framework of bourgeois class interests lost its specific historical significance, which of course varied considerably from class
to class or stratum to stratum. The Rockefeller Report* suggests
that the modernizing impact of external interests can take on a reformist meaning comparable to other purely nationally focused
impulses of bourgeois and petit bourgeois radicalism, either conservative (like the changes desired by the industrialists) or demagogic
(like the pressures toward consumerism and increased popular participation, from professional politicians). When all this diversity of
interests and values was crushed by class fear, the common reaction shifted the historical frontier to an ultra-conservative accommodation which no longer reflected the relationship of the dominant classes to the transformation of national society, but a new
relation more nearly expressing what all the possessing classes
jointly desired, namely the *status quo*. The stimulating and constructive interlocking of national power structures disappeared, to
be replaced by an impoverished likeness that identified "defense
of the system" with an egoistic mopping-up operation.

Thus, these two perspectives show how counter-revolution
first unleashed and then hindered, in one quick historical movement, the most dynamic long-term effects of the processes of unification and concentration of the interests and power of the bour-

---

The Rockefeller Report on the Americas (Chicago, 1969).

geois classes. No one can say where these processes would have led if they had continued to operate freely. What we do know is that they were broken off in an early phase (though they had been going on for almost a half-century) and that they culminated in processes of self-affirmation and appropriation of privilege by the bourgeois classes and their substrata, a result which contributed nothing positive to the differentiation and reintegration of the existing competitive social order. On the contrary, they strengthened processes that sociologists such as Max Weber would consider negative for the consolidation and further development of this system, or which positivist sociologists like Durkheim and the North American specialists in applied sociology would call pathological or sociopathic. Indeed, no sociologist, whatever his sociological orientation, can be unaware that counter-revolution had shifted the center of political gravity of the bourgeois classes and elites from its focal point in the relationship of the dominant classes with the integration and equilibrium of the national society, to the internal equilibrium of the bourgeois classes and their control of national society. We have already discussed, in the light of the recent changes undergone by class society, why this became historically "possible" or "necessary." Now it behooves us to point out what this development set into motion, at least over the short term, over a period of time within which the various links and connections of power of the ruling bourgeois classes achieved their greatest political effectiveness, thanks to the existence of an autocratic bourgeois state as an instrumentality for the regeneration of morality and the established order.

Taking our analysis a bit deeper, we find that bourgeois consensus, resting on the foundations and following the movements described, changed its political significance once established on the political basis of decisions taken by the regime. In the end civil society paid its price for the stabilization of the system and was imposed as the true—and in certain respects the only—valid political focal point of the nation. Yet it did not merely function as a source of the system's legitimacy; at the same time it was its revolutionary nucleus, the point of arrival and departure for all political processes that translated into practice the revolutionary will of the ruling bourgeois classes and elites and the institutional governments which represented them. Outwardly, this seems a subtle transformation, a mere shift in political semantics. In reality, the step was a key one, not only the static effect of the political dynamics of bourgeois power, but the material embodiment of the collective sense of bourgeois regeneration of the preexisting competitive social order. In fact, the political counter-revolution, over the long term interrupting the political dynamics of bourgeois power, replaced them with others which were to grow and function in the immediate political context, created by the institution of a regenerated social competitive order and subjected to the revolutionary and institutional controls operative in this new order. Thanks to this rupture and to the abrupt leap it made possible, bourgeois consensus acquired its own political revolutionary space through which it became the embodiment of revolutionary will and, as a consequence, came to be identified with the legal and political order of the nation as a whole and by extension, to embody the national sovereign political will as invested in the autocratic bourgeois state. The sapping of the dynamic forces of the class regime as a result of the premature interruption of the two concomitant processes of unification and centralization of the interests and power of the bourgeois classes and their substrata thus obtained unforeseen and crucial political compensation.

What should be stressed is that these classes and class strata forged a unity which extended neither to the other classes nor to the nonbourgeois political structures of the nation, yet which conferred upon them the concrete control of the legal and political order as well as the historical possibility of imposing civil society upon the nation. This change, which set in incredibly swiftly, completely altered the sense of bourgeois hegemony, above all its political functions, neutralizing its artificial roots and shoring up its precarious sociopolitical foundation. In this way the bourgeoisie escaped the relative political immobility to which it had been condemned by its pattern of class solidarity and hegemony, since by superimposing civil society upon the nation it did put its own limited democracy on a par with an oligarchy of the ruling bourgeois classes. Varying and conflicting interests and values began again to circulate and to link up or repel each other. However, from then on their center of gravity was "closed" and was confined within the bounds of civil society, where bourgeois consensus was situated and constituted a social and political force. Like other capitalist states, democratic and otherwise, the autocratic bourgeois state had to contain and orchestrate all the tensions and contradictions that are inherent in the stratification of class society even when the dominant bourgeois minority is closed in on itself.

Because of this situation it would only absorb these tensions and contradictions through the bourgeois consensus, which came to express directly its own internal "hell" and indirectly whatever was happening to the other classes and the nation as a whole.

This means that the bourgeois classes and their substrata emerged from the relative political immobility in which they found themselves to carry out what may be called a severe "politics of class," within the limits of which it could expand, given the framework of an "open" political and legal order, undermined, however, by the superimposition of civil society on the nation (or by a democracy limited to a class oligarchy). The political ties among those "more equal than others" were thus automatically degraded because the legitimation derived from bourgeois consensus was imposed, through the autocratic state, in place of the legitimacy which should have derived from the consent of other classes and national consensus. That is the crux of the matter. The political ties among those more equal than others, democratic-oligarchical in their essence and their actions, assumed directly and irrevocably the form of a systematic and generalized cooptation. This cooptation has occurred among groups and factions of groups, strata and factions of strata, classes and factions of classes, but always entailing the same intrinsic and inevitable corruption of the resulting system of power. Further, this cooptation has become a vehicle through which the diversity of interests and values in conflict has returned to the political scene, entrenched itself, and acquired support or rejection. In this regard, the bourgeois autocracy has ended up as a typical limited democracy which may be called a "democracy of cooptation." The result has been that the unification and centralization of the interests and power of the bourgeoisie have become consolidated, but have now taken a direction previously obscure (although perhaps it had been latent in the plutocratic substrate of bourgeois consciousness). With all its limitations and inconsistencies, the composite and complex pattern of bourgeois hegemony has thus displayed its utility as a bridge between the national and foreign bourgeois classes, a flexible link which has facilitated the distribution of all those within the "revolutionary" political space and the uneven flourishing of power and advantages among those more equal than others. Thanks to it, the middle strata have gotten their share and gained privileges far beyond their own social prestige, moving the levers of the state apparatus, which is in the hands of the bureaucratic, technocratic, and military bourgeoisie. At the same time, and likewise thanks to it, the "really strong interests" and "predominant interests" found their ideal political medium and are now able to impose themselves at will from above and to flourish unhampered. If there has ever been a bourgeois paradise, it is Brazil, at least since 1968.

A critical sociological assessment of the autocratic bourgeois model of capitalist transformation must take these aspects into account from the outset. They pose for us the problem of total and absolute class dictatorships, controlled by the bourgeoisie and concerned exclusively with the preservation of capitalism and the capitalist state. But with a special characteristic: this is dependent capitalism, in the era of total imperialism, at a moment of world crisis at the periphery of the capitalist system, and taking part in a life and death struggle for the survival of bourgeois rule. Other bourgeoisies, even those completely conforming to the classical model of the bourgeois revolution, could be stigmatized for their egoistic individualism, their aggressive parochialism, or their "rational" violence. Even with all this, however, those bourgeoisies never lost sight of the dynamics of a class regime and the political socialization required for embedding class relations in a national framework. Both realities were incorporated in class interests, consciousness, and solidarity, and in the patterns of bourgeois class domination. They were manifested in egalitarian, democratic, and nationalist impulses that brought both radicalism and bourgeois consensus into a constant interaction with the interests and values of other classes and with the fundamental needs of the nation as a whole. Here we are faced with a dependent bourgeoisie that is struggling for its own survival and that of dependent capitalism, both of which it confuses with the survival of "Christian Western civilization." In the hands of this bourgeoisie, egoistic individualism, aggressive parochialism, and rational violence are directed exclusively toward the continuation of the economic pace of the bourgeois revolution—in other words, the intensification of capitalist exploitation and class oppression, without which that pace is impossible. Moreover, this is the sole point toward which the most disparate and contrasting bourgeois interests and values converge, to constitute a single historical pole at which all the "live forces," national and foreign, of the bourgeois revolution in dependent capitalism are united. Either the "acceleration of economic development" or the "end of the world": this is a historical truth which retains its validity, since the acceleration of economic development and its impossibility are the two extremes that unite the persistence of dependent capitalism and its ultimate destruction.

However, in a country with the geographic, demographic, economic, sociocultural, and political characteristics of Brazil it is not possible to maintain this static correlation between acceleration of economic development and safeguarding of the *status quo* "for all time." It might indefinitely be maintained if the bourgeois classes were able freely to accelerate economic development and at the same time keep the preventive counter-revolution going.[6] However, Brazil does not appear to be a propitious field for a solution of this type, which would require a "static association" between the two processes.

In the Brazilian situation there is clearly a strong contradictory relationship between these two processes. The acceleration of economic development—especially in the form required by intensive industrialization and the abrupt transition to monopoly capitalism—is tending over the middle and long term to throw the entire system of social classes into convulsions. The abrupt changes taking place are affecting both the conditions for differentiation and reintegration of the classes—*all* classes—and their relations of mutual accommodation, competition, and conflict. It might be assumed that unequal internal development would impede this phenomenon or at least slow the pace at which it has been developing since 1967. However, even at the cost of the anarchic congestion and crowding of the cities, or other parallel sociopathic effects, the acceleration of economic development has made the realities of the class regime much more virulent and irreversible than before. By contrast, the preventive counter-revolution is not a structural process endowed with comparable sociodynamic possibilities. Not only is it a local historical process already on the wane, it also collides head-on with the new relations between the bourgeois classes and their substrata and the new emergent competitive social order, revitalized by intensive industrialization and by the upsurge of monopoly capitalism. With each passing day it tends to diminish the unity among all the bourgeois classes and to drive bourgeois interests further apart, in particular those that are growing on account of this new competitive social order. While its profoundly reactionary direction coincided with the class fear prevailing in the heat of the crisis of bourgeois power and during the most acute period of "revolutionary regeneration," today it can no longer adapt to the rationality of capitalist transformation, speeded along from without and within by private initiative and state intervention. As a consequence, the processes of differentiation and concentration of the interests and power of the bourgeois classes have resumed their course, and at a much faster pace at that, thanks to this acceleration of economic development. The counter-revolution is not only being diluted, it is losing its material basis in bourgeois class relations and is once again becoming the expression of the economic, social, and political force of the ultra-conservative bourgeois strata, which have been thrown into relative disarray by changes in the bourgeois world and in class society.

Yet this contradiction has not effected a "political decompression" or "normalizing of the system," such as might have been expected in another historical context. On the one hand, certain factors involving a hardening of the order are not purely internal. They are imposed from without, as part of the world confrontation between the capitalist and socialist systems—a reality that has remained with us despite the incipient tendencies toward "peaceful coexistence." On the other hand, the contemporaneousness of the two antagonistic revolutions mentioned at the beginning of this chapter condemns the bourgeois revolution and the forces feeding it from within to permanent friction with socialism and the forces shaping it as an emergent historical reality. In fact, the disintegrative forces of capitalism are intrinsic to the structure of class society and tend to expand along with that society. In this respect the acceleration of capitalist development has brought about what the bourgeoisie most feared: it helped class society to expand abruptly and thus to augment the volume and potential of these forces, which had been repressed but were visible and feared. Between these two persistent determining factors, aggravated by the repercussions of the crisis of dependent capitalism, grew the need to arm the class society with police and military forces which could fulfill "within the order" (hence within its "normality" and "legitimacy") functions equivalent to a preventive counter-revolution, hot or cold.

This process has not yet been brought to completion in Brazil. Nonetheless, it clearly situates the political significance of the autocratic bourgeois model of capitalist transformation and makes patent what type of bourgeois hegemony it "normally" requires, i.e., as a permanent historical reality. Class dictatorship is neither contracting nor becoming diluted; it accompanies the development of the capitalist productive system and the class society that corresponds to it. With the situation under control, active defense of the order may be mounted without the "organs of security" requiring any tactical support from a climate of civil war; but this is maintained through police and military repression and "political compression." As a consequence, the preventive counter-revolution, which disappears at the historical level of direct forms of class struggle, reappears, concentrated and institutionalized, as a social and political specialty of the state apparatus. Here, in our opinion, is the room for forces conducive to political decompression, which has been fostered time and time again by the bourgeois classes since 1969 within the bounds of the "defense of the revolution." To achieve this end, the bourgeois classes would have to have a static as well as dynamic control over the system, and this, moreover, would have to be solid enough to enable them to neutralize the antibourgeois forces within their ranks or within the other classes. It would also have to have a "surplus of power" stable and strong enough to permit the hardening of the order in certain permanent, localized dictatorial functions of the "constitutional state" and, given this condition, to permit the undermining of the order, which cannot be attenuated or interrupted under dependent and underdeveloped capitalism, to continue for an indefinite period. On the whole, the "democratic progress" of these forces of political relaxation merely reformulates the political problem of bourgeois hegemony in terms of a new historical context, under a compelling necessity to forge organic links to join the mechanisms of a democracy of cooptation to the structures and functions of an autocratic state.

It may be concluded that openings are being made in two directions. This will not bring bourgeois democracy but the consolidation of bourgeois autocracy, because it aims at extending the democracy of cooptation, opening it up from below, to give access to sterilized—or sterilizable—dissidence, and because it wishes to define the limits of the surplus legitimate power which must be conferred constitutionally and legally on the autocratic state. It is not a question of a return to democracy—that never existed—nor of an attempt to open the way to an authentic democratic experience. What the bourgeois classes are seeking is something quite different. They would like to create normal conditions for the smooth functioning and growth of the competitive social order. Indeed, that order had been already established before 1964 and had been convulsed at its ideological foundations. It was revitalized in its economic, social, and political foundations by accelerated economic development and the preventive counter-revolution. The bourgeois classes cannot go further. To do so, they would have to let go of many things that in the final analysis are essential to their survival in a dependent and underdeveloped class society afflicted by two simultaneous crises—one rooted in the bankruptcy of capitalism, and the other resulting from the upsurge of socialism at the periphery.

The bourgeois classes will not, and cannot without destroying themselves, relinquish their privileges, their internal class controls, and the control they have over the working classes, the masses, and the national foundations of the structures of power. The privileges are at the root of it all, for if the bourgeois classes were really to "open up" the economic, political, and social order, they would lose at one fell swoop any possibility of maintaining capitalism and preserving the intimate ties existing between bourgeois rule and the monopoly of state power by the hegemonic strata of the bourgeoisie. The controls that are now turned inward on the "bourgeois world" are becoming much more resolute than they were in the recent past. As the preventive counter-revolution fades and perhaps even vanishes, bourgeois hegemony will have to find quite different links. The bourgeoisie will have to, with increasing urgency, supplement the routine mechanisms of direct or mediated class domination with new formal class controls, in particular coercive controls implemented by the state. Moreover, bourgeois radicalism will once again rear up its head, with the difference that now it will reveal in a more unmistakable fashion the other face of bourgeois radicalism, namely, a radicalism against the system. The most characteristic feature of the recent evolution of the competitive social order was the rapid differentiation and the tremendous growth of the middle classes nation-wide. There has been an "awakening" not of the masses, but of the middle classes. In political terms the dilemma posed by this turn of events is that Brazilian society has neither the resources nor the socioeconomic potential to administer to the "revolution in expectations" which has occurred and is spreading among the "minor league privileged." Finally, the democracy of cooptation, as it opens its ranks from below to various kinds of dissidence or challenge, gives rise to special problems of its own as far as control of the established order is concerned. Mechanisms of vertical social mobility and of corruption help to extend the frontiers of "bourgeois consciousness" and the "bourgeois condition" into the working and destitute classes. However, in a class society that is in a state of turmoil, human migrations, social and cultural uprooting, poverty, and social disorganization inevitably breed social unrest and frustration on a broad scale. For this reason we shall soon be experiencing a protest movement within the order "corrupted by the system" and protest against the order, a truly revolutionary protest, both typical of a modern class society. The bourgeois classes, therefore, are trying to move along with this historical turn, preparing themselves and the autocratic state for a future replete with difficulties in which they will have to confront for the first time manifestations against the system in the specific form of organized antibourgeois violence.

As far as we are able to go in our analysis and interpretation, there can be no doubt that the only way that the contradictions between the acceleration of economic development and the preventive counter-revolution can be resolved within the order is by a recrudescence, rather than by a weakening, of bourgeois despotism. It would appear beyond doubt that the most conservative and reactionary bourgeois classes will find that the price they will have to pay for the survival of dependent capitalism through the democracy of cooptation is too high. Yet this is the only path compatible with the type of "democratic opening" they intend to put into practice. On the other hand, despite the obvious similarities, it would be dogmatic to insist that the bourgeois autocratic state is no more than an underdeveloped and modernized variant of Fascism. By all appearances, even the transition to Fascism would be held back by class fear, which has so far blocked any form of ideological and political mobilization of the masses within the ambit of the preventive counter-revolution. The emergence of Fascist features was limited to the state, and was concentrated within some of its structures and functions, assuming thereby the character of a localized and institutionalized process (and symptomatically disguised and placed above any communication or linkup between the elite and the masses). There is nothing to indicate that the "normalization" of the autocratic state may take any other course. Finally, the bourgeois classes will not be able to count on conditions for confronting stage by stage the long-term process that would result from the marriage of such a precarious (considering its socioeconomic base) democracy of cooptation with such a structurally and functionally complex autocratic state. Possibly this marriage will, together with certain tendencies toward the stability of the existing order, intensify frictions within the bourgeois classes and between them and violent and ultra-leftist antibourgeois radicalism, which in modern societies is bred exclusively within these classes. It should be added that a democracy of cooptation has little effectiveness and "flexibility" in poor capitalist nations where the extreme concentration of wealth and power leaves a scanty surplus to spend on the purchase of alliances or loyalties. Hence, it ends up exacerbating the intrinsic contradictions of the class regime, driving them to the point that they weaken rather than strengthen the autocratic state, compelled as it is to function under the extreme, permanent, and self-destructive tension of an insurmountable armed peace.

In accord with the logic of these observations, the bourgeois classes may well, in spite of everything, pour more water on the mill and end up being submerged by the political process they have set into motion, by linking the acceleration of capitalist development with the autocratization of the competitive social order. In the emergent historical context of class relations and conflicts, the autocratic state may come to serve as a focal point for the advent of an authentic state capitalism, in the strict sense, while the systematic resumption of antibourgeois pressures and tensions could precipitate a revolutionary disintegration of the established order and the emergence of socialism. In either case the autocratic bourgeois model of capitalist transformation is condemned to a relatively short life. Both symptom and consequence of a much broader and deeper-going crisis, it will be unable to stay above that crisis and survive its resolution.

Translated by Michel Vale

NOTES

1. See Rosa Luxemburg, *The Accumulation of Capital*, part 3, *passim*.
2. See Paul A. Baran, *The Political Economy of Growth, passim*.
3. In the editing of the preceding chapters no effort was made to avoid a certain amount of repetition, which was due to inevitable overlappings in the analytical objectives or arguments. We felt that the reader himself would see the reasons for such an approach. Nonetheless, the mode of presentation we elected to follow has in some cases resulted in overlappings and repetitions within a single chapter. We have tried to minimize the inconvenience this creates by retaining only those repetitions that seemed to have a certain empirical or theoretical interest. In order to avoid making this chapter too long, we

have not attempted to discuss the convergences and discrepancies in any further detail, and accordingly have left to the reader the task of tying together the various strands of our rather loosely arranged presentation. Indeed, our viewpoint and conclusions are spelled out explicitly enough so that no further burdening of the exposition is necessary.

4. The same type of impact occurred with regard to the working and destitute classes. We feel it is unnecessary to discuss all the aspects of the situation in the present paper.

5. Hobbes used the two concepts in their classical, contrasting sense. However, we should like to stress that, as regards the implications of the second term, we have in mind Franz Neumann's important study of Nazism [*Behemoth: The Structure and Practice of National Socialism*].

6. Leaving aside the alternative of a "democratic consolidation" of the system, it is clear that the democratic bourgeois model of capitalist transformation is out of the question.

REVOLUTION OR
COUNTER-REVOLUTION?

In 1964 a military coup established a political regime in Brazil in the name of "revolutionary ideals." In fact it was a counter-revolution. The counter-revolutionary character of this regime may be understood in terms of its internal significance and from the perspective of the global situation.

Internally the regime emerged as a counter-revolution in a specific sense. It was hailed as the "self-defense of a democracy confronted by international communism." But such a conceptualization is a mere ideological cover-up of the true character of the regime, a manifestation of the most grotesque kind of political propaganda. What the regime attempted to head off was the transition from a restricted form of democracy to a democracy of widened participation. Though many have said so, this did not augur some kind of "populist" or "mass" democracy. Rather, the real threat came from a bourgeois democratic regime in the throes of consolidation. In such a democracy various sectors of the working classes—and even the more or less marginalized masses in both city and countryside—could count on a growing political space proper to themselves. Putting an end to and reversing this process, i.e., eliminating this political space which would allow for the direct or indirect participation of the working classes and the masses, meant not only putting a brake on the revolution within the established order but reestablishing the *status quo ante*. In other words, the so-called "democratic franchise" would only be effective for the possessing classes and their political elites.

From *Contexto* (São Paulo), no. 5, 1978. This is the abridged text of a lecture given in the autumn of 1977.

From the external point of view, the coup d'état was part of a broader process, in which the cold war and the doctrine of "development with security" were carried from the center to the periphery of the capitalist world. The capitalist net not only enveloped the authentic threat of a "communist subversion of order" but also, in the name of the "defense" and the "interdependence of the West," paralyzed a great variety of national revolutions. Thus, modernization in general, and democratic transitions in particular, were subjected to a tight political and military-police control, thereby banishing the working classes and the masses from the historical scene. However, it must be emphasized that this external impulse was not limited to the mere approval and support (though vital) of counter-revolutionary manifestations from within. In fact, the center brought to the periphery an urgent and at times chronic need of its own—to undermine and destroy the ongoing revolutionary political changes which could not be contained at the level that would benefit only the conservative and reactionary classes. The intertwining of these two tendencies can be seen therefore as expressing the depth of a worldwide counter-revolution. In such a scenario, Brazil emerges as a nation that is vital to the "security of the Western Hemisphere." Such reasoning cautions us against viewing the situation from an internal perspective only. It liberates us from the false hopes based on the elections of 1945, the Constitution of 1946, and the events that characterized the early sixties.

The coup d'état emerging from these two movements terminated an agitated though superficial period of expanding "bourgeois democracy." It was of course a bourgeois democracy proper to Brazil, a country of colonial origin, only recently evolved from a regime of slave labor and still very much a prisoner of imperialist domination. The coup did not pick up the threads of past political patterns. On the contrary, a new kind of class dictatorship required its own dictatorial state, which I have designated the autocratic bourgeois state.[1] As I pointed out, the class dictatorship and the dictatorial state do not mean that history has come to a standstill. Repression and oppression never had the power to "paralyze" or to "freeze" history. Indeed, by its very nature, the bourgeois autocracy cannot "endure forever." Capitalism, whether in the center or the periphery, imposes rhythms of rapid social transformation. These rhythms are even more rapid (and dramatic) on the periphery, where the internal contradictions of the class regime are aggravated by the contradictions inherent in imperialist domination. The center imposes a dependency on its associated bourgeoisies and on their states, the bastions of their strength, inhibiting their actions historically and blocking their structural development. Thus, paradoxically, the same conditions which precipitate the counter-revolution contain the seeds of its weakness and decline. Independent of any direct pressure from the working classes and the masses (who are no less present in history: a threatening presence aimed at the break-up of the autocratic bourgeoisie and the autocratic bourgeois state) and even before the front line of this direct pressure is felt, the articulation and the control capacity of the counter-revolutionary force are undermined by its own internal and external contradictions. All this indicates that containment by means of violence is limited to a short time span (perhaps ten to thirty years, which is very little in the history of peoples), and it must be exercised with extreme rapidity, intensity, and rationality by the counter-revolutionary forces. Now, this did not occur. Neither the countries of the center and their superpower nor the capitalist countries of the periphery could exploit this period of time in a "specifically preventive manner." Contradictions that have been aggravated over the years come back with great force and demonstrate the failure of the more recent style of dictatorial regime (a military-civilian composite, maintained by the Brazilian Armed Forces and the deterrent power of the hegemonic capitalist nations and their superpower). The regime is rapidly ceasing to be a guarantee of political stability, which must now be achieved by other means. If not, new nightmares will emerge.

This poses a new problem, one that must be analyzed if we are to understand the powerlessness of this capitalist net of global counter-revolution. In its least problematical aspect—the internal process of the counter-revolution caught in its own trap—we find bourgeois domination to be strong enough within Brazil and sufficiently flexible in its relations with imperialism to decide how the passage from the "revolutionary" (read: "counter-revolutionary") situation to a "political opening" (the capitalist "rule of law") is to take place. Insofar as the direct pressure of the working classes and the masses is not the principle factor in this transition, it is determined, regulated, and contained by the class interests of the ruling classes and their various factions. The actors in this drama could not continue with the farce. Nevertheless they could convert it into comedy, perchance attaining their goals by means of this "relative security" and not by means of a "relative democracy."

This is of course the heart of the matter. The ruling classes both inside and outside of Brazil (though in an unequal manner, which cannot be debated here) no longer perceive the dictatorial regime as a guarantee of *political stability*. While they are not about to let power escape from their fist, since they are not forced to do so, they try to adapt this concentration of power to the "normal channels" of political life. Not that they pretend to *revitalize* the parliamentary system. They know only too well that "normal channels" would mean a return to a democracy of broad participation and hence the "risk" of the reappearance of working-class and mass and their own political demands. In fact what they want is to transfer to the parliament the gradual search for an alternative system and the political responsibility for this task. This crippled *democracy of force* would merely prolong the concentrated class dictatorship and the counter-revolution, though in a less blatant and less visible manner, by "institutionalizing" and thereby legitimating the counter-revolution itself. Current political language needs no decoding. "Self-defense of the state," "relative democracy," "political safeguards," etc.—such terms are no more than a litany of clearly counter-revolutionary intentions, which have not been challenged head on by any truly counterbalancing social and political force. In effect, the madness of those who have the power goes on. Nevertheless, the scenario is changing. Those who put the nation on the Procustean bed are now called to give account of what they did and why.

The present discussion should focus on the substantive themes related to this seeming crescendo of historical oscillations. The counter-revolution ought to be the axis of this discussion since it continues full steam. The first theme follows naturally: what is this erosion of the counter-revolution and what does it portend? We then proceed to a connected theme: to what extent can the social forces of the counter-revolution condition the actual recycling of the political process? If we are not to be the victims of these forces a second time—first at the time of the coup and now at the moment of recycling—we must begin to ask questions that lead us to a confrontation: how to annul the impetus of these forces and create political space for the antagonistic forces which would pick up the threads of the democratic revolution and strengthen it?

The erosion of the counter-revolution was inevitable, first, because it did not generate its own "transition period." That is, it did not resolve any of Brazil's "great problems" in the intervening years. On the contrary, when we dissociate the political tempo of the national revolution (which was already in process and continues its development in spite of everything) from the economic tempo of capitalist development (accelerated as much as possible in order to respond to the rate of exploitation of surplus value and accumulation imposed by monopoly capital), we can perceive the counter-revolution as antisocial and antinational. It is antisocial in terms of the expropriation of labor, the exportation of the national surplus, the intensification of economic inequality and, consequently, the aggravation of social tensions (though this intensification is not visible on the surface and is mystified by a show of "generalized prosperity"). It is antinational in terms of its eradication of radical groups, the union movement, and the political vanguard of the working classes from *political society*. The coup either crushed or seriously weakened the fragile political dynamics linking the nation to the state and impeded the formation of the new political dynamics that had appeared as a democracy of wider participation was being consolidated.

On both levels, divergent or antagonistic class interests become more polarized, even though still merely potential. Since privilege based on the organization of the economy or on state policy feeds only private interests, the positive capacity of bourgeois domination to attend to the interests of the working classes and the masses is undermined. The autocratic bourgeois state has not been giving to these strata with one hand what it takes with the other. In fact it takes with both hands and gives back so little that there is no way to reconcile nation and state within the order created by the counter-revolution. The cleavages were deepened so rapidly and continuously that the bourgeois classes have lost the ability to enter into a political "dialogue" with the working classes and masses within the present order and through the mediation of this state. Seen from this standpoint the erosion is both structural and historical. It can only be overcome by a recomposition of an order which eliminates all those evils generated by the present regime either directly or indirectly. This, moreover, must be accomplished as quickly as possible. This means that there can be no half-way solution in the form of concessions and subterfuges if the divorce between the nation and the state is not to lead inevitably to civil war.

Second, by its very nature the counter-revolution is a military-political solution. Indeed the counter-revolution was made possible by the coming together of the possessing classes through their vanguard of economic, political, cultural, military, legal, and police elites (and in a certain sense, religious elites also) to create a political equivalent of a *sacred union* of their common interests. Sectoral conflicts were either set aside or covered over. The defense of "private property," of "private enterprise," of the juridical and political order which guarantees both, etc., surfaced and was given priority. Disparate internal and external interests could now be articulated. Moreover, a sufficiently solid class base made possible the use of civil war to block the democratic revolution.

Though the cold war was extensive, because of the peculiarities of the class structure in Brazil the hot war was limited. Had pressure from below been stronger and more identified with the goals of a democratic revolution (within the established order or against it), then the civil war would have taken a different turn and had different consequences. In any event, it effectively blocked the shift from a restricted democracy to a democracy of widened participation. Still more decisive for the possessing classes, they were enabled, though few in number and not well articulated nationally, by means of civil war to impose their tyranny. Even so they justified it in "revolutionary" style, with mystifications like the "defense of order," "protection of the democratic regime," "redoubt of Western Civilization and Christianity," etc.

Many conventional or formalist political scientists think that complex processes such as these are poorly perceived because it is only in advanced "civic cultures" that the masses have the cultural development necessary to perceive (and disapprove) such a reality. Nevertheless, the contrary has happened. On the one hand, since the counter-revolution legitimated itself of and by itself, there was nothing subtle about the transformation. That the possessing classes were protecting themselves and their privileges was clear to everyone, even the "least cultivated of spirits." The common sense of "second-class citizens" was all one required to see the political significance of what had happened in all its fullness. On the other hand, the militarization and technocratization of the structures and functions of the state were also highly visible. The fact that preexisting imbalances and inequities were aggravated was clearly due to the counter-revolution. Consequently, not only did the people (or "public opinion") turn against the dictatorial regime; much of its support—forthcoming for precapitalist privilege, the "defense of order" and the consolidation of the hegemony of monopoly capitalism—was also alienated.

Undoubtedly there was an unequal distribution of the dirty jobs: the military and the technocrats "dirtied their hands" in exchange for highly debatable advantages. Through skillful manipulation by the most powerful in the private sector, a negative visibility was focused on them. But that was not what was essential, nor does it capture the reprisals and the decisive tensions. The counter-revolution was born in fear, based on the panic of the possessing classes. But when this moment had passed, the solidarity of these classes could not be maintained nor strengthened on so heterogeneous and fragile a base. The chronic weaknesses of the possessing classes developed within the political and historical framework of the counter-revolution, undermining it continuously, inexorably. This did not impede the hegemonic sections of this class from pressuring for a "gradual" and "secure" normalization. However, it does mean that even those sectors, when the initial period of panic is past, begin to look outside and above the "common interests" of the possessing classes for a solution to their dilemmas—and also to the dilemmas of class domination and of the state-political power of the bourgeoisie. From this angle, the "erosion of the counter-revolution" can be seen as a specifically bourgeois problem. Since the counter-revolution was unable to generate a solution to the crisis of bourgeois domination and the political problems intrinsic to a dictatorial capitalist state, it was forced to sacrifice itself in the short run. The Trojan horse was not outside but inside the walls of the bourgeois fortress.

Third, wherever the political and economic tempos have been dissociated, the political stability imposed *manu militari* was not intended to serve the nation or for that matter to serve all sectors of the possessing classes equally. On the contrary, the problems that had to be confronted on the periphery of the capitalist world were (1) how to accelerate modernization with its typical "revolution by incorporation" and at the same time keep the control of this periphery in the hands of the hegemonic capitalist nations and their superpower; (2) how to maintain the political stability which was a prerequisite of the global operation of the multinationals or the larger corporations and to further their growth in these "strategic" dependent capitalist nations; (3) how to prop up the hegemonic sectors of the possessing classes within these nations as a "national" business community or administrative and political state "bodies" associated with imperialism. In general, the larger capitalist nations on the periphery were gathered in this net of determinations, as can be demonstrated in the case of Brazil and Mexico. On this level the counter-revolution was no more than, and could only be, a pragmatic instrument aimed at the achievement of short-run goals—at times, those that were consumed *in actu*.

While the more conservative and reactionary strata of the possessing classes tended to see the sacred cause as a permanent counter-revolutionary process, their more dynamic forces perceived the process more in terms of a surgical intervention. It may be added that the external conditions of the counter-revolution could not be predetermined, since they were dependent on the totality of factors in the global capitalist economy and their evolution. The more dynamic forces wanted a modernization that would be at one and the same time "secure" and "rapid." They understood the nature of an "economic miracle" induced from outside and tied to highly unstable and uncontrollable external conditions. Repeated experience showed that they could "generate" such a miracle and "heat up" the economic process only for short periods. What then follows is that capitalist development is left to its own fate and has to obey the rhythms and limitations of the debtor nations.

This discussion illustrates the complexity of reality. The "economic miracle" as a typical and topical phenomenon never "comes to stay." Its collapse is as unexpected as was its appearance. Dissensions and mutual recriminations follow in its path. The counter-revolution is undermined not only by normal cyclical patterns but also by its own side effects. In the wake of the deflated "miracle" discontent rises even in the midst of the possessing classes. Resentments based on the unequal partitioning of privilege and booty cannot be stifled. The counter-revolution turns on itself, initially on the economic level and then on the political level. This passage from one level to the other can take ten years, a quarter of a century, or more, depending on the socioeconomic and political vitality of the receiving nation, but when it reaches a certain political level the erosion of the counter-revolution becomes uncontrollable. The possessing classes themselves become factors in its decomposition.

Fourth, this alliance between possessing classes of unequal force (and hence unequally privileged by the counter-revolution) results in the creation of an autocratic bourgeois state with several faces. There is a democratic face tied to the efficacy of a restricted democracy and indispensable to the functioning of the contractual order inherent in capitalism and its form of labor. There is an authoritarian face connected to state action, which must absorb various functions of accumulation and protection of profits, as well as intervene directly in the infrastructure of the monopoly economy by fixing the "rules of the game" and occupying certain "economic vacuums." There is a fascist face related to the coexistence of a ritualized constitutional and legal order and an effective institutional order, through which the class despotism ceases to be an "emergency" response and becomes the *sine qua non* of political stability.

This multiplicity of faces is informative. A class society that creates this type of bourgeois state generates a political element that makes it intrinsically unstable. The formation of such a state reflects contradictions that cannot be reconciled on the economic and social levels and which for this very reason are absorbed by the state, thereby converting it into a Frankenstein's monster. The contrary tendencies found in society now operate within the state and are amplified. Having absorbed and rearticulated social forces of unequal weight and character without at the same time simplifying them or eliminating their contrary aspects, the state which was at the mercy of the potentialities of the "common interests" of the dominant classes now stands at the mercy of their debilitating "common interests." The more powerful protagonists (such as the multinationals, financial bourgeoisie, large "public" or "mixed" enterprises) and those holding key strategic positions (the civilian and military technocrats, the *great electors* of the regime) tend to prevail. They struggle to reduce the political space and the voice of weaker protagonists (the agrarian and agro-industrial commercial interests, the small- and medium-sized industrial bourgeoisie), the petite bourgeoisie, "traditional" middle classes, small- and medium-sized commercial strata), not to speak of the working classes and masses, who are excluded from the status of protagonists in the "institutionalized" political process.

Though it appears a monolith, the autocratic bourgeois state is debilitated by sectoral conflicts within its own ranks. These conflicts cannot be annulled or restructured. The economic and political costs of such action would undermine the viability of the regime itself. From this standpoint—which though the least visible is undoubtedly the most relevant—it is clear that the state, the basis of the counter-revolution, is ultra-vulnerable. The autocratic bourgeois state is a giant with feet of clay. Just as its imposition was *natural* (as a historically created reality) so too is its erosion. It advances gradually to the top of the hill only to roll down the other side with extreme speed to its ultimate collapse.

This point is fundamental. A civil society whose most powerful and active strata constitute a privileged and ultra-privileged minority compared to the mass of the population and the size of the nation, offsets its sudden force (which accounts for the success of the counter-revolution) with a corresponding insuperable weakness (which explains its failure). The economic base of the autocratic bourgeois state is much too narrow. It is a prisoner within a restricted civil society. Locked into the defense of its own privileges, it is incapable of attending the interests of the nation as a whole or of maintaining its own capacity to hold on to the "sacred union." It is clear that the impasse resulting from these three faces can be (or could be) overcome in a number of different ways, many of which are quite compatible. Nevertheless, the relative autonomy of the counter-revolutionary state is undermined by the weight of interests of the more powerful internal and external classes.

Every dictatorial state generates a certain political autonomy which is crucial if it is to realize its built-in goals. In the case of those regimes that were born with the spread of monopoly capitalism to the periphery, the superimposition of the three phases victimizes the counter-revolutionary state. It is unable to harmonize those interconnected structures and political mechanisms in a perpetual or even long-term unity. To the extent that institutionalized repression and oppression are concentrated and intensive, it is capable of preserving a static equilibrium of the institutional order. However, the very counter-revolutionary forces of order undermine this equilibrium bit by bit. It is impossible to reconcile their aspirations for greater and greater relative advantage with the necessity of reinforcing the autonomy of the autocratic bourgeois state.

In other words, this state, independent of all "pressures from below" (it is clear that the appearance of such pressures precipitates the fall), gradually loses all possibility of forming a dynamic connection between the spheres of state action, civil society, and political society. It is curious that those who hold the reins ignore this phenomenon and behave as if nothing had changed or could have changed. It is possible to outline this process and its direction by pointing to the various protests and opposition movements based on the interests referred to above. In Brazil these ranged in form from the "loyal opposition" ritually reserved to the "opposition" party to those manifestations specifically directed against the autocratic bourgeois state and prohibited by it. This is the significance of the student protest, which broke the chains of domestic or indirect control; of the intellectual protest, wherein lawyers, journalists, priests, professors, actors, composers, etc., dissociated themselves from the conservative pressure which had hitherto paralyzed their professional associations; of the disquiet among certain entrepreneurial groups who were less and less inclined to follow the institutionalized routes of communication with the government; etc.

Pressures from below continue to be repressed. Their appearance is sporadic (wildcat strikes, sabotage, wage demands, etc.). All political space continues to be monopolized and occupied by various sectors of the bourgeois class. Nevertheless, this is of little importance. Because it is precisely at this level that the erosion of the counter-revolutionary and dictatorial regime proceeds, those who created the monster now intend to devour it. It is from within the ranks of bourgeois interests, from the citadels of bourgeois domination that the first attacks on the "redemptive" counter-revolution come. This demonstrates that the Achilles' heel of the autocratic bourgeois state is to be found in monopoly capitalism itself. Nevertheless, this also means that the possible political "openings" are defined by that same source! The possessing classes have not so transformed themselves in the last thirteen years as to be converted into their own historical antithesis.

How could the champions of counter-revolution convert to a radical-liberal bourgeoisie in the short span of thirteen years? How could a timid and pro-imperialist bourgeoisie metamorphose into a revolutionary or "conquering" bourgeoisie? The link with monopoly capitalism gives us the clue to the political equation. The shift is from an autocratic bourgeois state to a "rule of law," but the latter may not and cannot be a negation of the former. On the contrary, this shift is supposed to establish a capitalist state "normal" for Brazil and "ideal" for the times. It is to be an instrumental state, its goal being to bring about a *strong democracy*. This is the extent of the shift. It can be seen that the substantive change falls short of the semantic change.

The questions raised by the second theme lead us to a similar conclusion. In the mortal confrontation with socialism, capitalism has only "poor" alternatives to offer. If this be true for capitalist nations of the center, it is more so in the case of capitalist nations on the periphery. Caught between their terror of a socialist revolution (the rebellion of the masses against the established order) and a destructive avalanche of unlimited imperialist domination (which "internationalizes" precisely that political space which pertains to the dominion of the local bourgeoisie and internationalizes some of the structures and functions of their own bourgeois state), the national bourgeoisie on the periphery turns away from the real path to autonomy, a democratic revolution.

This is a situation which mirrors the central drama of capitalist civilization. It survives by the reproduction of the existing order. It advances by means of a technology which gives capitalism great flexibility in terms of brute force, mass consumption, and unrestricted pollution (nature, human beings, culture—nothing escapes). Hence a *threatened capitalist civilization* contains an immanent counter-revolutionary residual which grows and multiplies on the periphery, where the great numbers of the "wretched of the earth" have reached the point of swamping the few "privileged beings." This means that the savage capitalism of the periphery has its own intrinsic political rationality: it leaps from traditionalism to ultra-revolutionary modernization. With "modernity," bossism is converted into authoritarianism without the mask. This transforms the character of bourgeois despotism. It ceases to be a rational domination by means of ends and values, and is transformed into a domination which is openly autocratic. It is as if civil society were militarized in terms of an elitist professional ethic. Such a generalized counter-revolutionary residual breaks down the barriers among all technocrats, whatever their social or economic location.

This counter-revolutionary residual must be analyzed within the historical reality forged by the coup d'état of 1964 and the regime which it originated. In the context of the last thirteen years, this component of recent capitalism appears to be at the crest of total exacerbation. The heavy industrialization of Brazil is not merely an event sponsored by imperialism and state intervention. It takes place under the tutelage of sullen and hidebound "bossism," supposedly metamorphosed into "bourgeois rationality," which is committed, not to the defense of the existing order and a democratic revolution, but to the imposition of this regime by means of force and organized violence—that is, by means of a counter-revolution euphemistically called an "institutional revolution."

It is important that we analyze the process that leads to this typical and topical form of tardy bourgeois revolution. It is equally important that we take note of the fact that counter-revolutionary forces in an explosive class society have taken the center of the stage, acquired dominion over the nation and direct control of the state. To summarize, a blindly conservative bourgeoisie depends on an autocratic bourgeois state as a third armed hand, repressive and oppressive. Though bourgeois formulas and the autocratic bourgeois state are greatly undermined, one reality inexorably emerges: a democratic revolution will not take place through this form of class domination which has become the sacred means for the defense and reinforcement of capitalism. It must either transcend this form or it will not take place at all. The conclusion is obvious. The counter-revolution will not give ground. It is prepared to impose itself by means of mystifications and camouflage. Capitalist rationality has been so perverted that it is now natural for it to confuse the "institutionalization of the regime" with "political opening," "relative democracy," and even "full democracy." A phantom, the rule of law, is resurrected. It cannot count on a Bismarck, not even on a Prussian nobility. Nevertheless, the bourgeoisie itself absorbs all possible roles: it tears apart the robe of political society and produces the democracy that suits it.

The current recycling through which the regime is passing is clearly designed to prolong the "institutional revolution" by other means. It is either this democracy or nothing! Hence the whole phraseology concerning strong democracy, a rule of law equipped with the means of self-defense, etc. This simply means that the forces of counter-revolution intend to conduct the recycling in accordance with their own interests and designs. Their enemies are frightened. For the present the working classes and the masses have been so far annulled that the revolutionary potential has been destroyed in the heart of their adversaries. These lack the courage to speak of democratic revolution, of confrontation or a counter-movement. "Bourgeois democracy" and "proletarian democracy" are objectively opposite poles in a democratic revolution. In this sense the word democracy has become a potential risk (when not a pure farce). This state of fear, this surrender in the face of struggle shows what ground we tread on. The counter-revolution is here to stay (this is the way to translate the current motto of its champions: "the revolution is here to stay"). Those who "direct" or "lead" the regime, those who are its "servants" or its "cadres" as well as those who make use of it or its "mass," are concretely, wholeheartedly, and arduously committed to preserving the regime from destruction.

However, what might be the difference, in terms of degree, between the present regime and this "strong" democracy, this rule of law equipped with safe-guards, etc.? Is there any chance that we may have seen the end of arbitrary rule and oppression on the part of those same counter-revolutionary forces which are now in power? After all, a transformation of this nature would be very convenient for the forces of reaction. They could continue to act freely and with impunity and, as good fortune would have it, without any negative visibility! The rule of law, tempered by the institutional acts* that have been "constitutionalized," would make an indefinite stay legitimate. The amended sonnet is worse than the original. The new regime would prolong the other, but we would sink deeper into the swamp. The people would remain outside of history. The nation, handed over defenseless, as it is today, would continue to be at the mercy of a combination of the powerful.

This brings us to the final theme. Having eliminated all fantasies of a "bourgeois democracy," is there no room for hope? We must not overlook the fact that under monopoly capitalism, class society is no less antagonistic for being repressive and oppressive. The view that conflicts have disappeared or are negatively selected in recent capitalism—in spite of the respect some champions of this idea, like Marcuse, might merit—ignores the fact that a socialization that deforms a population and external controls that paralyze a nation must one day confront the reaction which springs from a multitude of tensions and frustrated hopes. When one speaks of class society, one speaks of a particular history. In class society nothing is eternal, not even capitalism, its foundation and material support. By focusing our attention not on the center, but on the periphery, this key fact can be observed with greater objectivity.

Bourgeois autocracy first emerged in the periphery. And it is in the periphery that we can trace the patterns of its erosion and

---

*This is a reference to a series of decrees that gave the government, especially military tribunals, powers beyond those in the constitutions of 1964 and 1967. These included censorship, arbitrary arrest, and suspension of Congress. The decrees were abolished recently, but elements had indeed already been incorporated in congressional law. —Ed.

in the middle distance, its coming demise. Frictions, dissatisfaction, tensions are observable even among the possessing classes (isn't this a formidable paradox?). These generate a new antibourgeois sentiment among the offshoots of the bourgeoisie. There is impatience and shame—more visible and at times more radical among Catholic groups and the younger generation of the bourgeoisie. But we also observe a rejection. For the time being it is something latent and the circles affected by it are small though growing. But, if even Latin American Catholicism—till now drugged by traditionalism—and the privileged youth of the middle classes join the ranks of the disenchanted and those engaged in active condemnation, this is solid evidence that what today appears as the exception will shortly be the rule.

We return to the language of Engels. The laws of social science are historical. They explain the formation and duration of social structures: how they are created, how long they can be maintained, and why one day they have to disappear. Any such diagnostic can only render approximations. Nevertheless they are reasonable approximations which allow us to infer that that portion of humanity which lives under the rule of capitalism is not condemned, certainly not condemned forever. Taking this position in our interpretation of reality, it is possible to delineate those limitations which are not born of history itself but of the history possible under monopoly capitalism.

Hence the "inevitable" and the "unchangeable" exist only in the minds of those whose analysis of monopoly capitalism does not penetrate to its inner structure. From the standpoint of its determining causes, it too is a historical and passing reality. It can be confronted just like any other social formation of the past—no matter how brutal, inhibiting, and terrorizing the legal and illegal forces for the conservation of order might be—as long as one maintains a critical perspective. The only real question is the risks one is willing to accept. If opposition within the order already has the character of intolerable subversion, then opposition against the established order becomes a mortal heresy. Nevertheless, the first condition of an efficacious class antagonism consists in antagonistic reflection and then antagonistic practical action. Without these two interrelated aspects, a political space beyond that which is produced and reproduced by the "forces for the preservation of order" does not and cannot exist.

This discussion indicates what must be done. To begin with, there must be a semantic operation (essentially a political task).

The concept of democracy must be brought back from the limbo where it has been stored by counter-revolutionary forces. To accomplish this the mind must be liberated from the hobbles of a class totalitarianism that prohibits every egalitarian proposal for a *democratic revolution*; that is, every proposal that struggles against capitalism and imperialism. The so-called "democratic question" is located in this context. Even in those countries where civic culture, political participation, and mobilization are married to a system of representation, consensus, and parliamentarianism, the democratic revolution has been sterilized by a form of liberty which is polluted and made meaningless by social inequality. The situation on the periphery of the capitalist world is much worse—need we be reminded why? There is no use gnashing our teeth, only to swallow the poisoned saliva. We must begin with a new, forthright, and clearly stated platform. Why render to counter-revolutionary forces powers they do not possess (and never could possess)? They cannot annul our creative imagination, our political will, nor our capacity to repudiate and confront them. It is at this point that the abstract idea of democracy is distinguished from mass movements of democratic revolution.

Those who conceive of themselves as isolated and broken have lost sight of the historical perspective. Why have these thirteen years failed to quash the basic personality of all "men of the people," their desire for liberty and equality, their impatience? Why does a timid, fragile, and acquiescing opposition get the spontaneous support of the working classes and the marginalized, destitute masses?

In a country like Brazil the democratic revolution can only count on a very weak point of departure. But the challenge confronting us does not stem from this. It consists in creating a political space which can be occupied by the majority, composed mainly of workers, the destitute, and the marginalized. How can this be done when we live in a class society dominated, manipulated, controlled, and violently repressed by the most reactionary and *ultra*-reactionary of the bourgeoisie, who are firmly opposed even to the emerging (and inevitable) transition to a democracy of wider participation? *By not giving ground.*

The present path and direction of the counter-revolution must be exposed, its meaning clarified so that all can see why it must be thrown into the dustbin of history. In like manner, the meaning and direction of a democratic revolution must be expounded. How can we begin this journey? The theory that "the

worse it gets, the better" is not a viable, constructive, and revolutionary political conception. On the contrary, it is defeatist and
paralyzing. In our present circumstances we either begin to fight,
using all available means at our disposal with a view to consolidating greater and greater victories, or we facilitate the continuity
and supremacy of the counter-revolution. It is not necessary to
succumb to hesitations and compromises. What is extremely urgent
is to stop this infantile thinking which proposes that the masses
can be politicized without having to struggle. All struggle must
inevitably start with a political space equal to zero. Though this be
a weak starting point, it is the beginning of a democratic revolution which will challenge the political space currently monopolized
by the forces of reaction and counter-revolution.

Only such a beginning will make further steps possible, liberate new alternative reformist and revolutionary forces, and break
the historical enclosure in which the working classes and the popular masses now stand. When tactic and strategy are combined, the
question of democracy begins to be a systematic and generalized
defiance through civil disobedience. It is not enough to hold dissenting views; *struggle* is demanded. This can only be done through
firm and continued civil disobedience. Until now there has never
been an example of a minority-based dictatorial regime, strong
enough to maintain control of the economy, society, and state,
that gave way spontaneously and without a struggle. If the forces
of counter-revolution are to be eliminated, their impositions must
be systematically disobeyed. We must not fear its violence nor
concede any essential political ground. This has to be true both of
individual behavior and that of groups and classes acting on the national level. An autocratic counter-revolution must be confronted
by a democratic revolution. Once begun, it will spread and multi-
ply its forces. In this manner alone can the dictatorship of a powerful minority be negated here and now and a democracy, organized
by and for a majority, planted in its place.

Translated by Patrick M. Hughes

NOTE

1. See *A Revolução Burguesa no Brasil*, chapters 5, 6, and 7. [Chapter
7, "On the Autocratic Bourgeois Model of Capitalist Transformation," appears in this collection.]

THE LOST
GENERATION

The idea to write this little essay arose by chance. I never felt much at home with "generational balance sheets," and despite repeated readings of Mannheim, and the profound impression a text of Gramsci's made on me, I had always thought that intellectuals exaggerated the importance of this concept. Furthermore, our cultural history is marked more by influences from without than by internal continuities and discontinuities. Whenever I found myself forced to speak in generational terms I would feel a bit flustered, because I felt myself closer to those who were coming, and a bit ashamed, as if I were adopting an alien value by evoking an amorphous term of reference which seemed to adjudge my worth in terms of age and the significance of the positive contributions of others. My own state of uprootedness did not bind me to the past of the intelligentsia, and my own positions arose from abstract convictions and political ideas as well as an intellectual process— the growth of the social sciences at the University of São Paulo— which for me removed the need to identify myself with a specific generation or part of a generation.

Thus it was with strong intellectual and emotional disquiet that I faced what was for me a reality: the discovery that I belong to a *lost generation*, a group of intellectuals which accepted its role and in a real sense accomplished its tasks. Even so, it did not manage to achieve its objectives or see its talents put to good use by society. I would not say that our presence has been useless: indeed it has not, and that alone justifies this essay. However, our

From *A Sociologia no Brasil: Contribuição para o Estudo de sua Formação e Desenvolvimento* (Petropolis: Editora Vozes, 1977), pp. 213-52.

presence went beyond the possibilities of history, and though Brazilian society had need of us, at the same time it was unable to free itself from obsolete structures of power which clashed head-on with our attempts at an audacious "leap forward." As in an animated cartoon, the pond was emptied so fast that our high dive ended dismally, not to say disastrously. At the end of three decades or so, all that we aspired to do no longer has practical meaning. We see the new crop of youth re-embark along the same paths to redo what was already done, without their effort having the benefit of an advance that ought, at least, to have represented a new point of departure and a more mature and profound critical reflection on the relations between talent and society in Brazil.

The instance that gave rise to these reflections was a chance meeting with Costa Pinto. He was traveling from Waterloo to Kingston and had more than an hour's layover, with Sulamita, in Toronto's Union Station on May 15, 1976. He telephoned me to come meet him at the station for a little chat, which I did. At the moment of farewell, I felt as if this were our last goodbye and I looked back over our life, marked by the difficulties of our formative years and the beginnings of our careers under a dictatorship, capped off by even greater difficulties at the end of our careers under another dictatorship. Costa Pinto was also moved, and responded to my agitation, obvious from the tears in my eyes, by saying, "Lay off, old man, we'll still be seeing each other many times and we'll laugh at all this." However, that situation did not begin and end in the "there" and "then"; I found myself confronted with the dramatic reality of an atomization, a dispersion, which had put the final seal on a beginning full of promises and hopes. Having stifled and repressed for more than four centuries every outbreak of critical and creative intelligence, conservative thought finally succeeded in making a clean sweep and imposing, who knows for how long, its uninspiring pattern of intellectual sell-out and moral cowardice: a victory in reverse, which reopened the country to the enslaving and continually reinforced currents of cultural colonialism. It was this against which I was reacting and rebelling, with all the impotence of one unable to "purify the temple" alone. We three lost persons, wherever we were, dragged there for different reasons, were no more than a living testimony to the tenacity of an inquisitorial obscurantism that had plunged the Iberian world in both Europe and Latin America into a prolonged era of darkness.

As I waited for Ken Walker and Marion in front of the station, the idea came to me to try to describe this human situation, not so much to provide a "written testimony" as to join combat. I had to get to the bottom of the pit and re-emerge from it not with the bitterness of frustration and defeatism, but with an explication that would put things back into their proper places. A *lost generation* is not a defeated generation, and still less a useless one. Its importance grows if someone within it is able to advance far enough that it becomes necessary to expel the tumor. Yet we are still far from a settling of accounts; meanwhile, however, we must throw the windows open wide to let the air and sun into the cellar of our subterranean cultural world. Many will speak of *revanchism*. But revanchism of whom and against whom? Who believes us capable of succumbing to this gloomy inquisitorial obscurantism? We had already joined combat with it long before, with the arms of reason, and with open and candid intellectual debate. Now, we feel such great repugnance toward it that we want to see it buried. I do not accept this inversion of roles, which transforms the torturer into the victim and justifies oppression in the name of liberty. Those who proclaim "Christian faith" and the "defense of democracy" in order to unleash a blind counter-revolution are themselves the gravediggers of Christianity and democracy. I have nothing in common with them, and I am not in this cellar by any fault or choice of my own. Hence I am writing this essay as the last contribution that one of the members of this lost generation can make, to call on the minds of the age to return to reason and to state what had been our aims in the name of a legitimate and belated aspiration toward cultural autonomy. Those who come after us will be able better to judge what they must do and whether it is not time for us to free ourselves from conservative thought, with its Iberian methods of intellectual obscurantism, which indeed are even now being destroyed at their source, in the Portugal of Salazar and Caetano and in Franco's Spain.

It is not my intention to undertake a sociological study of a generation. It is too early for this. Moreoever, a generation is like a bag of cats—at least it includes cats of all colors. What I have been referring to as a lost generation is not a totality (of individuals, orientations, and ideas). We had our pharisees, our Pilates, and our Judases. These I have left to one side, some in sorrow, others with a certain fondness: comrades who went astray, who had not understood their epoch and their intellectual roles, who took up false arms, and who ended up ignorant of true combat, the correct field of battle, and the inevitable common enemy. In particular, they did not have the strength to maintain an independent faith in reason and a love of liberty. They succumbed to a self-indulgence, some out of cupidity, the majority out of alienation or because they were unable to abandon their conservatism, undermined by their family circle and by a class solidarity that had roots in four hundred years of domination by a slave and patrimonial order. I am not unaware of them and I recognize that, in speaking of a totality, they will have to be incorporated in the history that had to be. Nonetheless, they were not the courageous ones, those who were able to cry out "We shall never surrender!" Nor were they brave enough to refuse active collaboration (albeit often disguised) with those who made use of power to unleash an odious and destructive repression. They then became indifferent to those who had joined the intellectual resistance of self-protection and self-defense. The "we" of this essay, therefore, refers to a small nucleus of a generation taken as a whole: those who dared, before and after the advent of terror, those who staked out the psychological boundaries, the cultural aims, and the political field of this "whole," sometimes losing, sometimes retaining positions already conquered. Thus we shall be speaking of a segment of a generation which in critical terms could be called the "intelligentsia" in the strict sense—of the intellectual committed to his calling, militant for his cause, whether or not he had fallen victim to the hecatomb of the *cassados*.* With respect to this fragment of a generation, I shall be offering my own subjective vision of what we intended, of why we failed, and of the lessons we should draw for the future. This is perhaps not much, but it is all I am able to do, inspired by the idea that a process exists, transcending us all and continuing in its course, and that it is upon its direction that we should give heed.

What we intended

A significant fragment of a generation may be focused on from many angles. In this description I shall be concentrating on one of its citadels: the one in which I was educated, grew, and achieved

---

*Cassado: one whose political rights or right to teach or work for the government had been officially cancelled. —Ed.

intellectual maturity. I have therefore excluded any overall sociological analysis, as I have already said. I have also ruled out any
sociological analysis of what generally are referred to as "the great
men of a generation," i.e., in this case, the "representative figures"
of the nucleus of the intelligentsia that formed and consolidated
itself around the Faculty of Philosophy, Sciences, and Letters of
the University of São Paulo between 1940 and 1960. The time has
come, I think, for one of us to pinpoint what we had in common:
not *what was typical of the extremes*, but *that which was typical
in what was shared*, with varying degrees of intensity. Those who
came before, as was the case with Oswald de Andrade, who provided a way out of the distortions of the *Semana de Arte Moderna*,*
had a wrong and superficial, nay, profoundly wrong and superficial view of us. They exaggerated our "serious side," as scholars—
what scholars? Was there really a climate for scholars in Brazil, or
in the narrow-minded urbanized provincialism that was so quickly
exposed for what it was? They enjoyed calling us a "pain in the
neck" (*chato*-boys). Nonetheless, this fragment of a generation did
have one distinguishing and dominant characteristic. This was not
strictly intellectualist obsession, obsession with erudition for erudition's sake, however that may be understood; rather, it was *political obsession*. Viewing it from today's vantage point, I am able
to understand it better: it was a political obsession that was born
of the culture and contained within it, reaching out toward the
problems of the epoch and the dilemmas of Brazilian society, because an authentic culture demands a responsible interaction between the intellectual and his environment and his times, mediated
by the tasks born of the internal growth of that culture and its
spread throughout the society.

Our means and our ends came from this growth and from the
opportunities it opened up to us as actors in a history that moved
in fits and starts. The critical impulses, the participatory conception of intellectual roles, and the "taking of a responsible position," as it is called, proceeded from this central point, which ruled
out the polarization of the "*ridendo castigat mores*" of the modernist generation and puts us face to face with bourgeois morality
and bourgeois domination, with a decided "no" to art for art's

---

*An exhibit in 1922 which introduced modernism and futurism, giving rise
to an earlier generation of cosmopolite, sophisticated, and somewhat self-
deprecating intellectuals. —Ed.

sake, philosophy for philosophy's sake, or science for science's sake, as much as to political "do-nothingism," the tyranny of custom, and the conservative imperium of power. As a result, we developed a generally modest perception of ourselves, whereby we saw ourselves more as a link with those who came after and as *servants of a society* in the process of cultural transformation. This is what set us apart, even in relation to the recent past and the pervasive elitism that prevailed even during the pseudo-destructive outburst of the *Semana de Arte Moderna*. In sum, we were not scholars but professors committed to their profession, seeking in it and through it a way once and for all to break out of our narrow cultural orbit.

The paradoxical fact of this condition never ceased to torment us, and came time and time again to the surface and to our consciousness, thanks to three related elements interacting with our personalities and our actions (or our omissions). First, the political attitude I referred to earlier evolved as part of the unique Brazilian cultural situation and its specific historical context, which made that attitude an intellectual necessity yet at the same time repressed and frustrated it irremediably. It was not just the repressive apparatus of the Vargas dictatorship that was at work here. There was also an intramural battle against the conservative mind, since the University of São Paulo was dominated by the mentality reigning in the old schools of higher education and the world of letters was marginal or hostile to our struggle. With all our "professorial" modesty we were condemned to the aggressiveness, even if self-protective and disguised, of "black sheep." Perhaps for this reason we appeared "pedantic" or "arrogant," when in reality we were seeking allies for a "leap forward."

Second, this political attitude, in turn, was not so conspicuous as to be directly visible and recognizable as such, despite the known militancy of many of us in radical democratic socialist movements (initially clandestine, later open). For example, upon their return from Europe, the most outspoken representatives of domestic liberalism delivered the following opinion of us: "Too bad they have no political experience." This apparent "generation deficiency" did not exist, or rather it was a fiction. The elitism of the developing class society, its power extremely concentrated in the hands of the ruling classes, created its own definition of "political experience." And naturally only those had political experience who, apart from belonging to the highest strata, were themselves decision makers or possessed some portion of state political power. Even our direct involvement—for some of us relatively prolonged —in the subversive struggle against the *Estado Novo* did not qualify, since political experience meant "command from the top down."

This element was not merely of subordinate importance: it must be seen as fundamental. In the first place, it was not just one or a few intellectuals who renounced the roles of a cultural elite implicit in the liberal-conservative tradition. It was an entire group, relatively active and creative, which burst forth onto the historical scene with an attitude that fluctuated between indifference and irremediable hostility to elitism as a form of cultural domination and social monopolization of power. The fact that the political component of the predominant attitude was very minor was useful to this group, since as a consequence it was able to go much further as a generation in its destructive and constructive functions than would have been possible otherwise.

Third, the political attitude in question turned in on itself, i.e., it fed on intellectual aspirations and psychological and social impulses that could only exist and grow within a small group, within which it operated as the driving force of a subculture (in the anthropological sense). It remained largely uncomprehended and repressed from within, i.e., within the institution that should have supported and reinforced it and encouraged its continued growth, namely the University of São Paulo. And although from time to time it was superficially tolerated or temporarily supported from without by economic, social, and political groups that came into contact with us, these groups did not understand our goals nor did they fight for them: their "universe of discourse" was another, which made them markedly ambivalent in their attitudes and conduct regarding our intentions, over both the short and long term. There was no psychological or cultural basis for any fruitful ongoing dialogue. And even those who went furthest, in liberal-democratic and socialist terms, used us more than shared with us the values that defined our conception of cultural participation, democratization of culture, and the responsibility of the intellectual. They even regarded us as means for other ends, without compromising themselves or quite simply not understanding the importance of cultural reconstruction as central to any search for a new formulation and a new solution of the historical dilemmas we faced.

Thus on the whole the intellectual affirmation of this fragment of a generation was not focused enough to permit its two principal ambitions to be achieved. On the one hand, it had no roots and did not rest on truly firm ground capable of giving its political attitude an institutional framework that would enable it to endure, defend itself, and spread. On the other hand, it had no external pole to which it could relate and from which it could derive strength. The intellectual who is "used," even when he goes about his tasks zealously, does not on this account find greater support in behalf of his mission, which transcends the immediate objectives of the "others." Allied by chance, they remain true to their own logic in keeping separate the objectives of the intellectuals—however valuable they may be for the creation of a true university or for the growth of science, for example—from the objectives of the social movement or currents that mobilize them. To go beyond this narrow alliance, the driving forces of society as a whole would have to be more thoroughly permeated by, and more substantially dependent on the functioning of a real university and on the practical fruits of scientific research.

Nonetheless, these were the two irreducible weak points and points of frustration which shaped the mettle of that political attitude. Exhausted and weakened inside and out, it could only turn in upon itself, and seek within its confines and within itself the strength to exist, grow, and spread. Like the backwoodsman, above all else it had to be strong; the alternative was to be crushed or to be domesticated. We learned rapidly that our strength as well as our sense of duty had to come from within ourselves, dissociating our functioning as intellectuals from institutional or superinstitutional recognition. Without succumbing to sectarian attitudes, conduct, or mentality, we derived our vigor and the purity of our fundamental political identification from our physical apartness, our overall cultural isolation, and from an entirely abstract idea of mission, of relation to society, and of collaboration between successive generations. A psychologist would see in this response aspects of overcompensation and subjective radicalization. However, how could we evade the pitfalls around us, a constant menace to our work and its continuity—not to speak of our security, both personal and as a group—unless by some device with which to fill the inevitable institutional and historical gaps? Only a political attitude firmly rooted in the creative functions of the university, of science, philosophy, literature and art, and indissolubly identified

with the idea of a creative intellectual role, could generate stead-
fast convictions and overcome the lack of an organic and autonomous process of cultural development.

As a historico-cultural formation, this political attitude did
not appear just in São Paulo. Between the thirties and the mid-
forties it also emerged in other large Brazilian cities such as Rio de
Janeiro, Belo Horizonte, Recife, Porto Alegre, and Salvador. It
seems, however, that São Paulo presented the conditions of a bourgeois city *par excellence*, linking capitalist development to the
more or less typical cultural processes of the era of "modern industrial technology." The paths followed were not the same as those
of European modernity; nevertheless the political attitude inherent in the relationship of a critical intelligentsia with life and society appeared (or at least tended to appear) like that of Latin Europe, especially France and Italy, namely, the militant and responsible intellectual who practices his calling on a scale surpassing professional vanity, by situating the tasks of the intelligentsia in direct
confrontation with history as a living process. This sudden shift,
which wrenched the intellectual from monolithic conservative control and from the ideal of belonging to the elite of the dominant
classes, was not in itself the exclusive product of university education and the new intellectual preparation of the scholar. It has
much to do, directly and profoundly, with the historical context
of the city of São Paulo. There the contradictions of capitalist development, the clash of agro-commercial, financial, and industrial
interests, reached a critical climax. Various sectors of the bourgeois
classes, with external material or technological incentive and support, aspired to transform São Paulo into "the greatest industrial
center of South America." What is more, they believed that, without breaking the umbilical cord to imperialist domination, the impulse for this process could be fueled and guided from within, on
the French model of a national democratic bourgeois revolution.
The analytic simplifications of social scientists have not yet succeeded in dissecting the complexity of this historical situation, especially the merger of agro-commercial and financial interests with
industrial interests, and the extent to which the oligarchy in the
major urban centers of the state of São Paulo had ceased to be
purely traditionalist. Thanks to coffee and its direct association
with world financial capital, its businessmen transformed São
Paulo's oligarchy into a luxuriant efflorescence of dependent competitive capitalism. There was something of everything in it. The

predominant cultural horizon, however, was financial, and the archaic and traditionalist sectors of the oligarchy were just as bourgeois as its modern and liberal sectors. Despite the conflicts of interest and the disjunctures, it is meaningless to speak of a destruction of the oligarchy and an opposition between "oligarchy" and "bourgeoisie," as some interpreters of great intellectual merit are wont to do (Ruy Mauro Marini being the most important of these). Although a unification of economic forces did not exist, there was a convergence of economic, social, and political interests effected from without by mechanisms of finance and of commercial-industrial modernization imposed by imperialist domination. From within it was affected by the common experience of peril during the 1929 crisis and of new commercial and industrial opportunity on the road to economic recovery, by the real or potential threats of the labor movement during a phase of "national crisis" in the structures of power, and in particular, by the strengthening of the traditional and modern oligarchic sectors of other states—a most serious phenomenon for the bourgeois classes of São Paulo, since it imposed on the "locomotive that pulled Brazil"* external controls that undercut their autonomy and brought them to the verge of making disadvantageous political deals and economic bargains with former allies and long-time enemies. In fact the "liberal revolution" nationalized (in the sense of increasing the stability of national politics and state control of economic policy) the participation of the bourgeois classes in economic and political power. It broke the hegemony of the producers and dealers of coffee over importing and exporting, banking, and industry. In their reaction to this situation,[1] both those sectors commonly called "oligarchic" (which in fact joined together different types of plantation owners and businessmen, also of various types, in a heterogeneous liberal-conservative front) as well as those commonly referred to as "industrialists" (likewise of heterogeneous composition, including various kinds of plantation owners and businessmen, and also under the liberal-conservative leadership of a few bankers and industrialists) all moved in the same direction. They regained the control and hegemony they had lost by means of a swift and thorough cultural modernization, forming new intellectual cadres for the elites of the ruling classes. Thus São Paulo was to overcome the

---

*An expression by which Paulistas described their relationship to the other states, here obviously ironic. —Ed.

"backwardness of the country," thought of as a backwardness of political leadership and an inability to adjust intellectually to current needs. Thus the simultaneous establishment of the Faculty of Philosophy, Sciences, and Letters of the University of São Paulo, under the aegis of the first sector, and of the Free School of Sociology and Politics, under the aegis of the second. Thus the liberal-conservative reaction to the structural crisis of bourgeois domination in Brazil had a "long-term" component in the domain of cultural change. Their utopian illusion, rooted in inexperience, was that the historical framework for the development of cultural elites was static, and that the historical framework of culture could be modified without at the same time transforming the historical framework of society and of bourgeois domination.

We are not interested here in this confused state of affairs, which was to exact its historical price from both the bourgeois classes and the intellectuals and the institutions created to alter the quality of the cultural elites and their leadership capacities. What is of interest are the two poles of this dilemma: the institutions that had been created, and the city in which they were to grow. They are not neutral poles. On the contrary, in some Brazilian cities those institutions were quickly exhausted; in others they would not achieve the same success. Certain peculiarities of São Paulo, as a bourgeois city, were fundamental to the growth of these institutions. Not only had class contradictions reached the peak of ferment, they also prevented obscurantist pressure from imposing "house rules" or the guidelines of a "revolution in customs." For at least three decades, the institutions thus created enjoyed broad freedom to choose their own way within the limits imposed by the scarcity of material and human resources or by the lack of a rational plan for their organization, growth, and the constructive use of their results. At least part of the credit for this freedom must go to the elitist tradition. From the very outset, liberal-conservative utopianism tied innovation to wholly bourgeois designs of economic, cultural, and political hegemony. It would be necessary for events to demonstrate the initial error in order that the elitist standard of liberty might be submitted first to external criticism, and then to brutal intervention. In part, this freedom was born of the sheer inability of the elites of the dominant classes to understand what they were doing and to control a full-scale institutionalized cultural process. A number of times reactionary and obscurantist interests mobilized against innovation, even in the domain of state government, but were unable to achieve their objectives. Their own agents ended up identifying with the innovations and with the course of things, and exposing the intrigues. What should be brought out, however, are positive aspects: the city's economic and demographic growth, and the extent of its modernization. Within a process of industrialization involving the creation of links between a nascent metropolis and its hinterland as well as other regions of the country, the bourgeois classes were more immersed in business matters than in demonstrating what appeared to be their "citadel of modern culture." For various sectors of the bourgeoisie, the institutions were for the training of intellectual cadres, and were channels of social mobility (important for the middle-class "old families" and for the rich and moderately well-off immigrant families). Indeed, the institutions meshed at various points with the "cultural needs" of the bourgeoisie, and if little by little the initial intention to attack the stronghold of the national state was lost from view, the instrumental character of these institutions was made evident in various ways. Finally, one must not forget the stimulating effect of the contact among peoples of various ethnic and racial origins and diverse cultural backgrounds, and of liberal and radical ideologies or anarchist-socialist movements. This ferment affected not just the nonconformists at the "top," from the traditional families, who provided audiences for the most brilliant French professors. It also reached more modest sectors, the middle classes, and even the working classes, who saw in formal education not merely a means of upward mobility but also of enlightenment, survival, and political struggle.

Thus, the *institution*—we should say, the Faculty of Philosophy, Sciences, and Letters of the University of São Paulo, and the Free School of Sociology and Politics—should not be seen as an isolated phenomenon, in and for itself. It provided an island for the intellectual in formation, segregating him spatially and isolating him culturally, a situation that was irremediable but also productive; nonetheless, the institution still interacted with society. The city provoked it in various ways and, in the final analysis, it was for the city that it *functioned*—if not for the city as a whole, at least for the centers where the social forces of conservatism, reform, and revolution were most active, and indeed somewhat virulent as well. Consequently there was a constant tension and contrast between these two poles which must not be lost from view. The institution moved ahead through a complete and accomplished *cultural colonization*: the mass importation of foreign teachers, organized as delegations or in small groups, and later individually. This reflected not merely impatience and the acknowledgment of imperial power. First and foremost it signified an internal mobilization without precedent of the cultural resources of the capitalist countries at the center. For the first time, dependent cultural modernization began to organize and establish itself from within, and on a large scale. This was a *leap forward* (or suicide?) by trapeze artists without nets. We were those trapeze artists and it was up to us to decide what to do with the mass of imported culture. In what direction to go? We could submit to a colonial tradition (why not?) in which we might place at the service of the central countries the prestige they conferred upon us and the power accruing from accommodation to the overlapping interests of the imperial centers and the elites of the ruling classes. Everything had been orchestrated to this end, and the lack of independent intellectual traditions simplified the process—to which, by the way, some groups of intellectuals succumbed. The industry of prepackaged culture, so well known and so denounced in countries that had suffered the process on the same scale, to take Canada as an example, was still relatively unknown in Brazil.

The European teachers who brought us culturally up to date had an Enlightenment conception of their roles. They were concerned with neither the material nor the cultural base for the absorption of such a rapid and massive intellectual modernization. For them, students were students; and they presumed that the Brazilian student was prepared to receive what they had to teach. Nor were they concerned with the fate their influence was to suffer at our hands. Most of them even tended to define the relationship in static terms in which the Brazilians would rise to the intermediate levels, retaining the umbilical cord to the top, with the supply of teachers at the highest level to be continuously renewed by other foreign teachers. Only teachers who became naturalized, and a few others (such as Roger Bastide, for example), saw that the field was broad enough to permit a restructuring in which foreign collaboration would continue, albeit on other foundations. The world of the university, both inside and outside of science, is not "national," it is "international," and these teachers understood that it would take little to debase them with unwanted colonial mystification. We ourselves reacted in a critical way on two counts. First, we were critical because the experience had not been programmed and planned; it was put into practice without an eye toward growth and without any prior effort to build a body of institutions structurally and functionally adapted to the aims in mind. The innovations were swallowed up into an old organism or were abandoned to themselves, as occurred with the Free School of Sociology and Politics, which remained within a historical vacuum with no institution to fill in the gap. Second, we were critical because we imposed upon ourselves the task of absorbing a cultural pattern rather than being the servile hangers-on of a colonial relationship. The high quality of some of the professors caused a psychological and cultural panic. Few felt their equals, and even fewer felt that they could excel them. Nonetheless, an objective understanding of the cultural situation made adaptation easier: we saw that university education had to be retailored to fit the Brazilian student and our secondary schooling, and this task in itself invested us with constructive roles, enabling us to begin the process in our own way and to grow with it and through it. We also realized that all would be lost if we did not ourselves take it as our duty to produce knowledge independently, not imitating our teachers, but reproducing their style of work. That was the rub. What we had to absorb was not the content of their teaching but patterns of institutional organization, intellectual work, and cultural growth. This was where we had to concentrate our creative efforts: to transplant to Brazil the values, techniques, and institutions that would enable us to produce scientific, philosophical, literary or artistic knowledge in an original manner and with a maximum of autonomy.

All of this would have been impossible without the direct and indirect pressures, the intellectual and political drive of a city such as São Paulo. In practical terms, it compelled us to forge ahead, exploiting the conveniences of the colonial relationship and putting to our own uses all the cultural and political space that elitist inertia or tolerance placed within our reach. Indeed, those who make a diagnosis in terms of a rupture of bourgeois radicalism see only a part of the overall picture. The city engulfed us in this radicalism, for in São Paulo it seethed more wildly than in all the rest of Brazil. Nonetheless there were two other tensions of a different sort, which were at least as important for the way things turned out in the end. In the first place, the liberal-conservative temper and reactionary intrigues roosted not only outside of academic walls. The lack of resources and the counter-pressures originated

within the innovative institutions, victims of the tradition of higher
education and above all of the elitist orientation of liberal professionals. The conspiracy was not just a conspiracy of silence. To
"grow," these institutions depended on initiatives that required allies beyond the walls of the academy, not just among students but
also in newspapers, among "influential" persons or circles—the
formation, in other words, of a pressure group that functioned internally but drew on external sources for support and for the
achievement of our ends. In the second place, a number of nonconformist manifestations were not strictly of the "radical democratic" type. There were dissidents among the Catholics; there was
a kind of critical enlightenment among Protestants, spiritists,* and
Freemasons; there was a special antibourgeois nonconformism
among various sectors of the middle classes and in certain traditional families, both the powerful and those in decline; and there
was, in particular, an intellectual ferment produced by the partial
or total adherence to trade unionism, anarchism, and socialism,
which was hardly unimportant in a city with such a vast network
of trade unions, such a dense working-class population, and leftist
or "populist"** parties that attempted to mobilize the proletariat
and the popular masses and press their demands. To get an idea of
this vast panorama it would be necessary to study a movement
such as the campaign in defense of the public school, to determine
concretely how the intelligentsia established links with the diverse
economic, sociocultural, and political polarizations of class relations and class conflicts. While the springboard of democratic-
bourgeois radicalism was the changes taking place in the economy
and in society, the institutional dilemmas fused a radicalism that
revolved around a cultural revolution for science, for letters, and
for scientific technology, and antibourgeois radicalism was shaped
by multiple influences which linked the engaged intellectual with
working-class protest, the trade-union movement, and socialist ideology.

All this means that the liberal-conservative sectors lost control, at one and the same time, of the innovative institutions and

---

*Mostly followers of Allan Kardec, a mediumist popular in the middle class at
the time.—Ed.
**This term is used in the Brazilian sense: urban-based and demagogic politics,
basically elite-manipulated, dependent on personality enhanced by media cov-
erage, and lacking grass-roots organization.—Ed.

the intellectuals created by them. As these institutions evolved, they redefined their goals to respond to the pressures of the surrounding society in all its vast and complicated ramifications. The intellectuals in turn began to see their own roles through their own optic, which they persisted in protecting institutionally, attempting in this way to free themselves from the external control of conservative power and bourgeois domination in general. While they were not able to give rise to independent movements based on their own political options, they were able to join and serve movements that arose from the possibilities of the moment. We painfully witnessed the consequent process. There was a double underutilization of talent. Within the institution, students came to higher education lacking the educational conditions that would have enabled them to pressure society from below. Within society, the nascent nonconformist movements were orchestrated by timid personalities drawn toward populist demagogy and its fragile democratic-bourgeois radicalism, which was hardly capable of mobilizing the trade unions or the parties of the left, including the Socialists and Communists. Intellectuals could have gone further on these two levels, and a good number of them desired and were prepared to do so by virtue of their political attitude and their ideological preferences. They were thwarted, however, by the possibilities of the situation, which put the intellectual "up against the wall" without, however, creating true alternatives of "revolution within the system" or "revolution against the system." But saddest of all was the disjuncture between the two spheres. The intellectual could be more radical in his relations with society than in his relationship with the innovative institution, since there the power of conservative control was more concentrated and dangerous. As a result, a rupture occurred between the intellectual's profession and ideological preference. The university teacher who could be socialist in his public noninstitutionalized intellectual role could not maintain this ideological stance in his institutionalized public intellectual role. The environment was not modern enough to permit this further step, which would only occur later and then only for a short time, since it was cut short by counter-revolutionary pressures. The effect of this has been negative insofar as conservative, liberal, and radical-liberal ideological positions are tolerated, exposing students to a systematic barrage of ideologies that are compatible with the system, with conservative control of power, and with the so-called "ethical neutrality" of the intellectual, a thing totally incompatible with the political attitude of a militant intelligentsia.

In any event, the most active members of this intelligentsia advanced as far as they could in three different directions. First, within the institution proper they fought for the creation of a system of education, research, and an applied science truly appropriate to industrial civilization and scientific revolution. In this area the battles were protected by institutionalization, and debates were able to flow more or less freely, setting up a kind of relationship between the intellectual and the public that had not existed in the past (not even during the abolitionist campaign). Since the young were more accessible to these debates and since the nonconformists and radicals were most concerned about them, militant intellectuals captured a vast public through a forum that brought together all classes and sectors of classes. Second, at the level of the established order, where its ideal requirements were entrenched and consolidated, the intelligentsia endeavored to take advantage of every opportunity to exercise a "revolutionary pedagogy modulated by established interests." At this level emerged ideas that repositioned the cause of national and democratic revolution within an egalitarian framework. For many socialists, this entire debate seemed useless, and indeed it produced nothing but agitation. Nonetheless it was not unimportant, since it provided a pretext for discussions of democratization of wealth and power, cultural participation, and democratic control of the state apparatus that went beyond conservative distortions and mystifications. Given the vast majority of the poor, and the broad segment of marginalized poor, this focal point in the intellectual's positive contribution was truly important, although it never was able to tie into an effective mobilization of the masses, even for the "bourgeois consolidation" of a democratic revolution. Third, there was the level of open nonconformity, identified with the working-class movement, trade unionism, and socialism. In this domain, the split identity of intellectual roles prevented militant intellectuals from being at the same time masters in their profession, agents for the spread of nonconformity, and creators of socialist thought. Therein lay the most negative aspect of bourgeois contamination of intellectual work. It was not merely the conservative control of power and the risks of being eliminated that produced this effect. The prevailing tendency was to divorce theoretical consciousness from practical activity, within a characteristically liberal conception of things. As an accommodation, this tendency was clearly self-protective and it seems beyond doubt that these were the limits of toleration. None-theless, something more could have been done (or at least at-tempted) to prevent the burgeoning of critical thought from sepa-rating into distinct channels of scientific development and scientif-ic socialism. What remained was a lesson in courage implicit in the staking out of a nonconformity that challenged the established order and conservative control of power. But it is and was innoc-uous, and does not even merit being taken as a point of departure, as did the contribution made by militant intellectuals in the other two spheres. However we now assess this shortcoming—which was in many respects more *theoretical* than *practical*—one point is incontestable, and that is that the gamut of nonconformist af-firmation of the militant intellectual went far beyond the bounds of bourgeois radicalism. Indeed, even when the intellectual moved in this direction, following his own ideological options or sponta-neous social movements, he struggled for democracy as a life style, democracy with development and full participation, and democ-racy with popular control of power and of the state, and opposed limited democracy, which merely enshrined the despotism of the powerful, the perdurance of counter-revolution, and the exuber-ance of an autocratic state.

Why we failed

The purpose of this discussion is not to whitewash the faults and weaknesses of the "lost generation." To do so on the pretext of understanding a critical and militant intelligentsia would be to crudely beg the question. What remained implicit in the foregoing must now be made explicit, not, however, with the fallacious idea of a justification. What must rather be done is to establish limits and explain why a bourgeois social order at the periphery of the capitalist world encountered the same barriers in the cultural as in the economic domain. Imperialist domination leaves no openings. When it stops the pace of history at the economic level, it does so at the cultural level as well. The bourgeois classes either close their eyes before these two realities, or throw themselves into the fray to further their realization, since it is their sad lot to combine the abrogation of the national revolution with massive industrializa-tion, the acceleration of capitalist development, and inundation by multinational corporations. The dissenting intellectual, little mat-ter he considers himself part of the bourgeoisie or not, must take another road. To explain himself, he must begin with truth—not a part of the truth, but all of it. Yet to do this is not the same thing as to seek a justification. On the contrary, it is to set the intellectual within the circuits of class relations and class conflicts so that he may discover how and why, in a dependent capitalist society, even the critical and militant intelligentsia is impotent as long as the forces of change or destruction of this society are unable to consolidate themselves and work in a revolutionary manner, either giving birth to an effectively democratic bourgeois order, or setting the stage for a transition to socialism. An ultra-radical rhetoric of condemnation and expiation would be useless: the intellectual does not create the world in which he lives. He has already done much when he is able to provide assistance in comprehending and explicating the world as the first step toward actually changing it.

The simplest way out, of course, would be to appeal to the obvious. "Bourgeois ruptures" or "bourgeois contamination" of the militant intellectual would then be the root cause of all these impossibilities. But history is not altered by such an observation. Why were the "victorious bourgeoisies" in Europe and America able to put to use the critical and militant intelligentsia of their societies in processes of democratic revolution? Why, in a word, are "democratic revolutions" a historical necessity in some capitalist societies, but an aberration or even the end of capitalism itself in other capitalist societies? That is in a nutshell the question we must confront in the periphery*: there is a difference between bourgeoisies who create their own historical paces and rhythms and bourgeoisies who "import" them, projecting them onto an internal development whose structures and functions are already present in imperfect form, being part of a model of civilization that expands by diffusion, dependent cultural modernization, and imperialist domination. If this difference did not exist, capitalism would be the same everywhere and bourgeoisies would be identical, and "democratic pluralism," a system of checks and balances, and "division of powers" would be universal phenomena. But bourgeoisies are different, and this political underpinning of bourgeois domination is crumbling and disappearing even at the imperial center, in the capitalism of the large multinational corporations. In a

---

*An allusion to the center-periphery analysis begun by the Prebischean school at the Economic Commission for Latin America, adapted later by dependency theorists, and by Fernandes.—Ed.

dependent and underdeveloped capitalist society, the intelligentsia, however critical and militant it may be, either becomes submerged in the revolutionary socialist movement, if such exists, or is condemned to live out a farcical counterpart to the tragedy of the national bourgeoisie. During this period the national bourgeoisie reached its apogee: its symbols reigned everywhere, and its values exuded vitality. It *seemed* that it was going to repeat, under different conditions, past history in the present, staging a tropical version of the nationalist and democratic "great revolution." In the maelstrom of the cold war, while the international structures of bourgeois power were being reconstituted, there was no place for this restaging of the past. History moved rapidly onward, following the pace and rhythms of the multinationals, the capitalist superpower, and the hegemonic capitalist nations swinging from this condition toward a relative autonomy. The "revolutionary" nationalist and democratic pipedreams of the dependent bourgeoisies of the periphery, reaching the climax of capitalist transformation belatedly, were crushed on the threads of this endless gear. The internal historical paces and rhythms were demystified: the critical and militant intelligentsia would have fulfilled a constructive historical role *if* . . . "if not for history"? No, history begins but only on the condition that intellectuals have sufficient prowess to diagnose the situation they have lived through and the pathways that will enable them to go beyond the historical gamut of dependent cultural modernization.

A diagnosis of this sort involves observations of two kinds. On the one hand, the interpretation of the most general determining processes that plunged the intelligentsia into a historical scenario that it was unable to change on its own. Whether or not it liked the present facing it, or the future to which that present was giving rise, at this level the intelligentsia was struggling with the hard realities of life, which no one, poor or rich, weak or powerful, worker or intellectual, can escape. The fragment of a generation to which I belong did not make the mistake of an illusory transcendence of history. It did not try merely to transplant intellectual aspirations to the Brazilian context where they would have been unviable. On the contrary, it did what was within its reach to do and struggled tenaciously to reconcile dependent capitalist development with the cultural requisites of democracy, and to link itself up with mass protest and the socialist movement. If it went a bit astray in its discernment, this aberration was a product

of history, not of the perversion of a utopian intellectual radicalism. On the other hand, there is something positive in the way in
which this fragment of a generation defined, both abstractly and
in terms of practical action, the tactical and strategical tasks of the
intellectual over the short and long term. Not everything here was
as clear as the noonday sun: the ambiguities and waverings of the
historical situation created ambiguities and waverings in the relations of this fragment of a generation with *its* intellectual world.
Nor could it have been otherwise. Nonetheless, it is on this level
that abilities, both those tried and proven, and those that were
only potential, reveal what was intrinsically aberrant in them. In
his vacillations before an impotent bourgeois order, the intellectual
absorbed all the weaknesses and mystifications that he himself
condemned and he ceased pushing his abilities to the utmost. The
political attitude inherent in his position and in his intellectual
leanings was drained and sapped *before* or *without* having the
chance to establish itself as an implacable cultural force within the
limits of the historically possible. Basically, the militant and critical Brazilian intellectual gave in to his social condition; he did not
have the courage to repel, or relegate to the background, social interests and values typical of a middle class gasping for breath under the conditions of dependent capitalism and a model of bourgeois revolution that countermanded the historical tempo of a national revolution, adopting in its stead the pace of an accelerated
economic development under external control. The result of all
this was that instead of earning acclaim as the knight-errant of the
political attitude of which he was the projection and incarnation
at the institutional level as well as on the broader stage of history,
the intellectual became its principal victim. These then are the two
crucial themes of this part of our discussion.

As for the first theme, clearly there would have been no dis-
engagement between the fragment of a generation to which I belong and the internal circuit of history if the intellectual aims of
that generation had stopped at a simple acceptance of the innovations brought by dependent cultural modernization. These innovations were to take place regardless of our wishes. Industrialization
was proceeding at full steam and approaching a mass scale; greater
São Paulo and the Rio de Janeiro-São Paulo urban corridor were
becoming economic and cultural metropolises, and as dependent
monopoly capitalism became the order of the day, it was inevitable that a broad "modernizing cultural revolution" should take

place with wide participation of native intellectuals and the extensive collaboration of others from abroad. This general process ran the gamut from qualitative and quantitative changes in the educational system—including the "university reform" (students were quite aware that we were moving toward a technical university and, moreover, how this was coming about)—to the adoption of a new model of capitalist development that would require new institutions, and new techniques and values as well. Just as had taken place a number of times in the past, with each change in the way Brazil was integrated into the world economy, a parallel change took place in the way we partook of "modern western civilization." In a word, we have tasted of a variety of epochs and styles of cultural modernization, set off and controlled from the outside, and influenced from the inside by our capacity to grow, i.e., to absorb the economic, sociocultural, and political driving forces of the imperial centers. What had begun diffidently in the thirties and developed as a torrent in the late fifties and throughout the sixties, pulled up short in the most recent period of dependent cultural modernization, marked by the predominance of the large corporations (or multinationals) and by the use of the national state as the "political arm" of the Brazilian bourgeois classes. The difference from the earlier phases is that of magnitude and intensity: the extent to which Brazilian society must absorb the economic and cultural driving forces of the hegemonic nations, i.e., "internationalize itself," in order to incorporate itself structurally and functionally—and historically—into the periphery of world monopoly capitalism. The leap that must be made leaves no sphere of social life untouched, from the demographic base and the relations of production, to technology, science, education, health, security, transport, the organization of living space, mass consumption, mass communication, and the economic, social, and political structures of power. In a word, all human activity susceptible of institutional standardization and control, both productive and nonproductive, became enmeshed in the most modern version of capitalist industrial civilization. No individual, generation, or social class in Brazil was uninfluenced by this vast cultural transformation, however extreme his or its "marginalization" and "cultural isolation." The innovations resulting from this transformation inevitably affected the entire generation, not merely the segment to which I belong. But what made this segment unique is the way in which it initially reacted to this era of dependent cultural modernization and to the kind of submission it required to outside influences.

The ambition was to achieve a maximum of autonomy as swiftly as possible in the production of various forms of knowledge, at the same time observing certain universal criteria for adjudging the efficacy and originality of the knowledge obtained. A development in this direction would of course require that Brazilian society should be able to reproduce institutionally certain minimal conditions for the production and application of these forms of knowledge (that is, that if in divers areas Brazil were not merely a "periphery," a structurally and functionally heteronomic entity, but could operate under conditions analogous to those obtaining in the "central countries"). It turned out, as a matter of fact, that this objective was within reach in various fields of the natural and human sciences, and in parallel developments in general or specialized education, and that it could be consolidated, and later broadened even further. Often the influx of material, technical, and human resources from abroad simplified the process, although it was not dependent on this influx, as was proven especially in the social sciences and, more generally, after internal material, technical, and human resources began to be channeled on a rational basis into publicly funded national institutions. The great practical problem was maintaining a certain level of development. Once a certain high point was reached, it became difficult to sustain it on an institutional scale or spread it among analogous national institutions. It was clear that the available talent was sufficient for the "initial leap" and for further advances midway, so to speak, and that the rational regulation of means°and ends by institutions was less of an obstacle than had been presumed. The spectacular growth of the University of São Paulo, especially in the Faculty of Philosophy, Sciences, and Letters, where almost all the fields of human knowledge underwent simultaneous (although uneven) expansion, proved that an "underdeveloped country" could free itself from external tutelage through its own resources and on a growing scale, provided only it found a way to concentrate some of its creative efforts on the intensive production and effective utilization of human resources. As a rule, the obstacles emerged after the pioneer stage, when association or competition with foreign centers instigated work that was spread too thinly at an early stage, or work that was of scanty or no theoretical or practical significance to the country. On the other hand, it proved to be rather

difficult to keep up the pace of gradual specialization and development once established, particularly in areas where the turnover or
expansion of material technical and human resources was relatively low. This concrete situation, which displayed recurrent and
typical features in areas of intellectual endeavor, both scientific
and nonscientific, was abstracted from the Brazilian economic,
cultural, and historical context by analysts. But in doing so they
overstated their case. They tended to "evaluate" the relationship between means and ends and "institutional research policy"
in isolated terms, or at best focused on interdisciplinary areas and
on the university as a whole. True, that is where the problems
would crop up, but their causes were more remote: to consider
them in their entirety it would be necessary to relate them to the
way in which Brazilian society embraced the capitalist model of
industrial civilization. Could Brazil really absorb this model of
civilization in relatively autonomous fashion? During the period
we are considering were the preconditions of self-sustained growth
yet present?

Seen from this sociological perspective, it becomes apparent
that the radical fragment of a generation, no matter how great its
intellectual and political militancy, could do very little on its own.
Many say that "intellectuals are not alone." But where were these
persons when we needed them, or where were the "nonconformist
movements" when we were calling for their help? But all this is
secondary. What is essential is that ultimately the political attitude
of this fragment of a generation operated within a historical vacuum that either throttled it whenever it went beyond system stabilization, or sapped it of the forces it needed to survive and spread
whenever it managed to interact with the environment and maintain itself. Its strong desire to break the bonds of cultural dependence and create an autonomous culture was diluted in a historical context in which cultural forces were polarized and controlled
by the centers of external domination and by the conservative
elites of the ruling classes. As a result, the values and intellectual
production of this fragment of a generation had but a narrow basis
of internal (and in some cases external) support. History itself had
moved in a direction directly antagonistic to it, at least over the
short and middle term. The burgeoning intellectual activity that
was spreading throughout the country in the end came under the
sway of these cultural forces and was reshaped by them. To begin
with, two factors were at work: the capacity to act and take the

initiative inherent in external cultural domination, and the interests of the ruling classes, bent on tightening and deepening their alliance with imperialism and on extending bourgeois control of the state, in order to accelerate massive industrialization and internal capitalist development. The counterpart of this was an intensification of dependent cultural modernization and the technocratization of the creative functions of intellectuals. The result has undoubtedly been that intellectual activity has thrived to an extent that would not have been otherwise possible. However, there was a clear political price: it was deprived of *revolutionary* dynamism that might have carried it beyond the purposes to which science, scientific technology, and the university are put under capitalist relations of production during the period of transition to a new model of capital accumulation and social transformation.

The control of cultural processes from without and within by bourgeois domination reinforced the trend toward dependent modernization, making of culture a "new frontier," defining what sort of innovative thinking was to be tolerated. After the initial groping phase with the foreign educational missions the reactionary influence came to be increasingly effective. The elite began to intervene directly into educational and research institutions. They became increasingly intolerant of intellectual ferment, and imposed their own uninformed, obsolete, oppressive, and obscurantist criteria of cultural evaluation and of selection of ends. Interests much less open than those of "old São Paulo liberalism" interfered drastically with the broad cultural process taking place, with the aim of containing it, controlling it, and even lowering it to the provincial and reactionary cultural horizons of conservative thought. Obscurantist traditionalism and the reactionary temper erupted exuberantly, counterposing themselves to the promising leap forward of the intellectuals and submitting the whole of creative cultural production to ultra-repressive containment. Innovative thought had then to face a hard reality: its subjection to external control was compounded by a narrow political space constantly manipulated by the "forces of order," those inside the cultural institutions or others imposed upon them, including the police and the military. While the first course of events was negative in that it forced adaptation to dependent cultural modernization, the second development was worse, and the best that could be said about it is that it threw out the baby with the bathwater. It even reduced the potentialities of dependent cultural modernization, imposing normative and selective criteria which, in addition to being repressive and destructive, were much inferior and utterly commonplace in quality. If this were not enough, the political arena was entirely occupied by cultural provincialism and reactionary obscurantism, predominant among the elite of a country without economic autonomy and without its own cultural tradition. The intellectuals were compelled to make concessions that destroyed the very foundations of innovative and creative thought.

On the whole, then, the course of national revolution was cut off in the area of cultural change, forestalling independent cultural modernization by Brazilian intellectuals in accordance with the interests of the nation as a whole. Those who held sway, whose interests determined the course of events, chose their own direction and imposed it on the intellectuals, the universities, and society at large. As a result the intellectual efflorescence suffered a reverse: it gradually abandoned its initial high standards; it lost its revolutionary fervor, either through constraint or concession; and its role was changed from that of a springboard to cultural autonomy to that of an obstacle, resulting in a more complete cultural dependence and external cultural domination. The radical sector of the Brazilian intelligentsia did not lose its critical functions on that account. But it was consigned to the underworld of society, condemned to ostracism and impotence.

As for the second theme, it seems that the time has come to "take off the mask." No generation escapes the limitations of the society to which it belongs. In particular, if it is a class society, no generation can, by itself, make up for its weaknesses arising from class conflict, or its suffocation, if this is a historical reality. As long as capitalism reigns supreme, each succeeding generation can do no more than make its own contribution, which will vary in richness and revolutionary verve, in response to the irreconcilable antagonisms in which it is enmeshed, not by its own doing, but through its links with the outbursts and constructive violence of class conflict. Without this impulse, there is no "new message," no creative intelligentsia capable of moving past innovative thought to action. Seen from this angle, the Brazilian cultural situation does not have much to offer either as a historical point of departure or a historical frame of reference. Not only did the class regime disentangle itself from slavery and traditional oligarchic control at a very recent date, but the freedom to make use of conflict was not institutionalized with the bourgeois order, as occurred in some countries of Europe and in the United States; the use of conflict, a seigneurial privilege of the past, became a bourgeois privilege in the present. Although this limitation does not prevent conflict from erupting from below, it nonetheless restricts the historical field within which class relations control and fuel class conflict. This has meant, in turn, that the options open to each *generation* are vastly and inalterably diminished. The structural and dynamic give-and-take between classes, generations, and class conflicts had little meaning for the historical process, and intellectuals accordingly found themselves reduced to seeking artifices to open up a cultural and political space capable of promoting and encouraging genuinely nonconformist or revolutionary expressions of a creative imagination. These external conditions enable us to see why the intellectuals who came out of the University of São Paulo threw themselves so zealously into exploiting institutional life, with the political and cultural space it offered, for the purpose of innovating. In certain respects, these conditions marked the first time a generation experienced the possibility of protecting itself through spatial segregation and cultural isolation. The institution, under the disguise and mystified cloak of cultural elitism, introduced freedom of thought, a certain creative boldness, and even a breaking of the bonds of "custom" and "the system." It was not the bourgeois order which brought this freedom and these possibilities. They appeared as a consequence of elitism, of the fact that the institutions of higher learning always had been conservative institutions, and of the intellectual inexperience of the ruling classes at a time when the modernist explosion of São Paulo burst like a flash of lightning over so provincial a society, devoid of "bourgeois unrest."

Nonetheless, these conditions, which enable us to comprehend the progress made, were also the source of the impossibilities. An intellectual generation that blossoms under such protection is irrevocably condemned to be caught up in class conflict, either through abstract thought or through the limited chances of the middle classes to participate in radical bourgeois "movements of popular opinion." It becomes a prisoner of the institution that protects it and under whose auspices it survives and produces. Another important point must be added here: the majority of the intellectuals were of petit bourgeois or bourgeois origin. The most brilliant of them came from "old families," whether rich, well-off, or in genteel poverty. They were received as if they should belong or did belong to the elites of the ruling classes, either by position or achievement. This link was never taken seriously, because the "middle classes," since the end of the Second Empire, had considered themselves a source of nonconformist and revolutionary ferment. This is an ill-starred penchant, however, based on a terrible historical and sociological error. Wherever a class regime is just in the process of constituting itself in the midst of popular oppression and repression of the working-class movement, and the mystical-conservative cult of "social peace," the emergent middle classes are imputed a power to make use of competition and conflict, a power that they would not have even if they were fully developed and numerous. Completely forgotten are the ambivalence of the middle classes, who tend to gravitate toward the preferences of the ruling classes, as well as the *real* desires of the middle sectors, from the end of the Empire and ever since. Quite simply, they wanted to spread privilege around more evenly, to have access to it and to the power of command or decision which privilege conferred. When the issue is described in these terms, something none too flattering is brought out, namely, a middle-class radicalism that is formless, intrinsically opportunist, fragile and cowardly, and ready to accommodate to conservative or reactionary manipulation by the elites of the ruling upper classes. Forming part of this middle class with its "lack of political tradition," the intellectual was not disposed to draw a sharp and radical division between his position as intellectual and his class position. On the contrary, his class position was the material foundation for his ascent to, or maintenance or improvement of, his position as an intellectual. It behooved him above all to maintain or to acquire a style and pattern of life that transformed him into a prisoner of his class and his class situation. This second prison aggravated the first, because even today the situation of the middle class is very ambivalent and vacillating. A "puritan" and "nonconformist" intellectual radicalism within the walls of the institution, indeed! But not a radical intellectualism that threatened and undermined class position! Even keeping our description to the most obvious facts, we see why the entire generation did not become intellectually radicalized to the point where they could collectively assume the political attitude inherent in the militant portion of the critical intelligentsia and why basically there were so few who were truly and consistently nonconformist in thought, creative imagination, and action.

I am carrying out an analysis, not an autopsy. We therefore need determine only the final result of this convergence, at bottom so convenient, which reconciled "critical intelligence" with privilege and the advantages of class position with those of intellectual radicalism. It clearly did not prevent the critical intellectual from becoming spokesman for this radicalism, thus braving the stream with an extreme intellectual puritanism previously unknown in Brazil. But this split the critical intellectual in two, however much he had identified with and participated in the radical democratic or socialist movements, and held in check his one truly revolutionary impulse to break radically with the existing order and to struggle against it *as an intellectual.* He was condemned to a nonconformity contained and nourished by the existing order, and moreover largely confined to the specific domain of creative imagination and inventive thought. On the other hand, this convergence, despite its constructive effects at this level, clearly transformed the institutional base (in this case, principally the Faculty of Philosophy, Sciences, and Letters or other institutions which performed the same function on a minor scale) into a citadel of intellectual nonconformity which did not aspire to "attack society," but merely to provide it with an alternative mode of cultural transformation and self-awareness. The citadel did not and could not raise a battle cry. It launched a utopian appeal to those who wanted to hear the proclamation of a "new era of enlightenment," in which Brazil would enter into the kingdom of industrial civilization and democratic sociability. Finally, and what is really most important, this convergence established both structurally and dynamically a schism between the cultural roles of the critical intellectual. He was enabled to be one thing within the institution in which he practiced his profession and enjoyed a minimal basis of material security, and another thing on the broader plane of his relations with society, where these roles could and should have meshed more completely with the potentialities of class conflict and their implications for national revolution. In exercising his profession the intellectual could move ahead at the same pace as modern civilization, but in his relations with society he could be hesitant, avoid his responsibilities, or give only that which the organized nonconformist movements were able to extract from him, usually falling short of the pace and functions that a critical intellectual would have to assume for those movements to penetrate into the class conflicts of Brazilian society. This nullified or at least drastically curtailed the practical effectiveness of the political attitude inherent in the radicalism of the critical and militant intellectual. An intellectual radicalism focused exclusively on the exercise of the profession and only incidentally serving to generate social ferment cannot be a historical factor of "reformist" or "revolutionary" change. It may be instrumental in changing the constructive functions of the intellectual within his small institutionalized world or in the production of original knowledge. Further, it may be instrumental for certain processes of purely institutional change and reform, in the academic world, for example, albeit on a small scale, because class conflicts penetrate this world through the conservative choices of liberal professionals and hence block the innovative drives of intellectual radicalism. But it could not be instrumental for those social currents committed to democratic revolution, either capitalist or socialist. For that it would have been necessary for the critical intellectual to absorb regularly, both in his institutionalized and noninstitutionalized cultural roles, the reformist and revolutionary meaning of class conflict.

Therefore, however much we may relax the rigor of our analysis, we must conclude that the interrelation among generation, class, and intellectual activity engendered contradictions that the critical intelligentsia did not attempt to analyze and resolve. This residual and structural omission provides one of the keys to understanding why the bourgeois reaction, when it came, was able to lay waste so easily and so rapidly to the citadels of this intelligentsia, even to the point of making use of the "liberal" counter-intelligentsia which was operating from within to destroy the autonomy and security of innovative thought. The inclination to restrict the scope and historical significance of cultural roles to a "professional" commitment to the institutional sphere of reformist and revolutionary action gave rise to the illusion that one could struggle for democracy, development, and social equality on one level while ignoring the others. It also resulted in a fatal underestimation of the conservative and reactionary temper, which launched its violent counter-attack simultaneously on both levels. The conflict should never have been contained within the institutional level, and the "basic reforms"* should never have been posed separately from a democratic revolution of the economic, social, and political order. As an adequate response to the historical exigencies of the situation, the critical intellectual should have forged a radical intellectualism capable of breaking with conservative constraints and controls at the institutional level and at the level of national society as a whole, i.e., capable of forging effective ties between his calling as an intellectual, his civil condition as citizen, and the ideological polarizations that pervaded social currents and conflicts. It was not enough to beat at the doors of the "most enlightened sectors" or those "most open to the demagogic populist manipulation" of the ruling classes; of the students, the student representatives, or the student unions; of the trade unions and working-class organizations; of the radical-liberal and socialist parties; or of the liberal democratic press. The task was to unify the divers political attitudes of radical intellectuals— intellectual puritanism, nonconformity, the desire for critical intellectual action, identification with democratic revolution, and the promotion of the popular masses as a "historical factor"— hence converting them into the structural and dynamic groundwork of an intellectualism negating the bourgeois order, a radical intellectualism. It, too, could operate simultaneously, like the bourgeois reaction, both on the institutional level and at the level of the national society, sending the engaged intellectual into all the pores and crevices of society where conservative thought and the reactionary control of bourgeois power could be combatted and destroyed.

Whether to our liking or not, our reflections have brought us to an irrefutable and inevitable conclusion. With all its merits and positive accomplishments, the intellectual fragment of the generation to which I belong behaved like the rest of the same generation just when it was crucial not to imitate others and not to make concessions. It distinguished itself from the latter more in degree than in substance, but mainly in the specifically intellectual sphere and in its understanding of the roles of intellectuals (thus its promotion of the "reform" of institutions in which intellectual

---

*Refers to popular and party-supported campaigns from the late 1950s up to the coup of 1964, for land-tax, university, and other reforms. —Ed.

work was carried out), in the "legitimate relationship" of the intellectual with social currents and political movements, and in intellectual puritanism. On the other hand, while it may have been the only sector to come up with a lucid analysis of the nature and implications of the national revolution, showing how economic development should be linked to democracy and popular control of power, it did not have the strength to carry this lucidity to the necessary practical conclusion, to an unyielding repudiation of the bestowal of privilege upon the bourgeoisie, national and foreign, and of the established order. Not that it lacked the courage to engage in direct struggle—many did so. What it did lack was the courage to couch this engagement in the terms of a radical understanding of the cultural role of the critical intelligentsia and of a renunciation of bourgeois conservative control of that role. The omission thus took place at a crucial juncture: no one denounced clearly and firmly enough the tendency of bourgeois control to separate the cultural pace of the national revolution from its economic pace. This sent the country headlong down a course of development that was to destroy everything in its path, from the "citadels of knowledge" and bourgeois patriotism to democratic control of capitalist development and of the state. It accepted, with an astonishing lack of critical vision (an evil of which I need not accuse myself), a deceitful conception of *development-ism* which entailed an endorsement of the mystifying liberal belief that spontaneous cultural change would of itself provide the solution to all our ills. This acceptance also paralyzed the critical attack of intellectuals engaged within the democratic bourgeois limits of a "revolution within the system," as if in a class society such as Brazil there existed *reformist democratic forces* sufficiently strong to overcome the egoism and obscurantism of the ruling classes, who preferred to yield to external domination rather than face the risks of revolutionary nationalism. All of this made us easy and defenseless prey to counter-revolution, which crushed all the wishful thinking about conciliation between dependent capitalism, democracy, and national revolution and exterminated the intellectual legacy of a critical intelligentsia. Subsequent generations had then to start out from zero—moreover, under much more arduous conditions, since they faced an organized repression against innovative thought. They had to forge ahead in a climate of widespread mistrust of the militant intellectual and to overcome the political demoralization that still weighs heavily on the ability of the "man of thought" to take practical action.

Lessons for the future

Does history really bury the living? What must the radical fragment of a generation do when it discovers that it lost its chance because it had faith in reason and confidence in man? Their work reduced to nought, should the actors, too, come tumbling down with the scaffolding, or should it be said that these "lost tasks" are not for all that "condemned tasks"? This is the paradox that emerged without the knowledge of this fragment of a generation, and I believe that the general feeling, which I share, is that creative thought cannot accept being sealed up and forgotten. The dilemma today is to acknowledge that we have reached a more demanding scale of duty. It is not a question of "setting an example" or "maintaining the cause of freedom" in the minds of others. If a society needs the intellectual for this, it does not merit a critical and militant intelligentsia. Nor do we need to demonstrate that "we're still alive" and that terror does not destroy thought. All that is puerile. Although our condition has changed, our role is the same. It is for us to act as a critical and militant intelligentsia that is still alive.

In this respect the lessons of the past illuminate the present, teaching us what we must to do defeat conservative thought and counter-revolution. It was not a mistake to put our faith in democracy or to struggle for the national revolution. The mistake was another—to suppose that we could achieve these ends by traveling down the royal road of privilege in the company of the privileged. There is no reform that conciliates an all-powerful minority with a wretched majority. If the minority is not ready to make concessions, the majority cannot obtain or impose them and all roads are closed; *the nation is an impossibility*. Democracy and the national revolution exist only as myths, not as historical realities. That is the way things stand for us at the last moment of our "age of maturity." It demands a reply, above and beyond the old illusions and accommodations, a response that obliges us to go directly to the root of the matter and to come up with arguments that count. This may be the "last role" we have to play on the historical scene, but it is doubtless the most important of all.

What is the *root reason* for one who rejects the confusions maintained on the right by the "upholders of order," the champions of the "institutional revolution," and by the "ideologues of gradualism" and the champions of "the rule of Law" in the center? The root reason consisted in getting close to the majority and its economic, cultural, and political needs, placing the people in the center of history, as the mainspring of the nation and of democratic revolution. In an era of wasted words, one must avoid verbal orgies. What we must do is not to "struggle for the People." Our intellectual tasks are of another calibre. We must place ourselves at the service of the Brazilian People so that it may acquire as quickly and as thoroughly as possible a consciousness of itself and become able on its own account to unleash the national revolution that would install in Brazil a democratic social order and a state based on effective majority rule. It is not merely to complete the process of decolonization, interrupted by the institution of the national state and dependent capitalism. It is also to free Brazil from the chains weighing on free and semi-free labor, in the countryside and the city, and from a secular tyranny that has always obstructed—today more than ever—the organization of the nation as a community and the advent of democracy. A retracing of the paths of the "great bourgeois utopias" or the restoration of demagogic populist rhetoric are accordingly out of the question. During the epoch of transition to socialism, mankind does not propose for itself the ideas of nation and democracy in the style of Europe and the United States in the nineteenth century. The interests and values of today found the nation and democracy in the economic, social, and political equality of all mankind. This means that they condemn the freedom for some to be more powerful than others, and reject any "fraternity" that allows the individual to be reduced to a thing and the exploitation of man by man in the market place. At the periphery of the capitalist world, in sum, there will be no restoring of the dead past of the hegemonic nations. The terms remain the same, but the nascent historical realities are and must be diametrically opposed. The new idea of "nation" and "democracy" requires majority control of power from the outset with the ultimate goal, ardently desired, of the extinction of a rule of law that stifles national revolution and blocks democratic revolution.

Such a conception of the root reason frees the intelligentsia from its imprisonment in the conservative straightjacket of the existing order. In adopting this conception, the intelligentsia ceases to be instrumental and organic to the cultural forces produced or reproduced by the network of institutions of bourgeois power, and in the process its own political focus changes. It ceases to be "radical" by virtue of and as a result of its "mobilization for order" (it does not matter by which means or whether it is in the name of "democratic radicalism" or "revolution through science"), and becomes gradually but increasingly radical for reasons that are intrinsic to intellectual activity in the strict sense or by means of the linking of the intelligentsia with other cultural forces originating in other social sectors, in the working classes and the popular masses, as movements of "revolution within the system" and of "revolution against the system." This transforms intellectual radicalism into a structural and dynamic fabric woven of the cultural potentialities of the majority, into a radical intellectualism, and frees the creative intellectual functions and roles from identifications (or pressures) deriving not from the culture itself, or from various forms of knowledge and intellectual activities, but from interests, values, and methods of control by the dominant minorities.

What this amounts to is a total break, a break that cannot be supported and sustained if the militant and critical intellectual isolates himself from society or, more precisely, from the social forces that give a historical meaning to democratic revolution. The intelligentsia merely ceases to be the prisoner of certain general propensities and limits imposed from without by the institutional network responsible for the professionalization of intellectual roles or as a consequence of bourgeois and conservative socialization of the intellectual. To what point his newfound freedom will be useful for the development of culture and for untrammeled creative intellectual activity is something that depends on other historical conditions, in particular on the continuity and the momentum of the social forces of "revolution within the system" and "revolution against the system." The important thing to be understood in this sequence of events is that the intelligentsia does not move from one master to another as liberal-conservative thought would have it; it does not free itself from the tutelage of the minority and from conservative constraints merely to fall under the tutelage of the majority and the constraints of a supposed "irrationalism of the masses." This is an elitist chimera and a self-serving corollary of liberal-conservative thought. Contrary to what this reactionary cataclysmic outlook implies, through the process outlined above the intelligentsia begins preparing itself to take part in a new social order, an order of equality of all and for all, and to participate as one of the conditions and forces that will bring about this fundamental equality. In other words, its creative capacities—"progressive," "reformist," or "revolutionary"—hitherto repressed, negatively selected, or severely perverted as conditions and forces of the capitalist system of production, will encounter ways to develop freely within each intellectual himself. First, they begin to stimulate and bring to fruition the democratic element inherent in national revolution. Then they are converted into dynamic factors of a democratic revolution that can no longer be contained within the confines of capitalist society and a national system of power controlled by the class regime. At this point they have reached the climax of their constructive influence, operating as a cultural force for the transition to socialism and the consolidation of a socialist society.

One may ask: Does not this conception of the root cause presuppose a utopia, and haven't intellectuals taken this utopia from socialist thought? In traversing this route will not the intelligentsia merely be opting from among social forces and historical movements extrinsic to himself? Finally, does not this way describe a growing link between the intelligentsia and the working classes and its reformist or revolutionary movements? Clearly, yes. The answer to the question does not lie in choosing a false pathway of radicalism, which disassociates the critical and militant intellectual, with his constructive cultural roles and functions, from the "revolution within the system" and the "revolution against the system." That would mean the inevitable sterilization of creative imagination and inventive thought, since the intellectual, independently of his abstract identification with radicalism, would continue to be at the mercy of bourgeois control, whether institutionalized or not, direct or indirect, "compensatory" or not. However, once the decision to accept the path described has been made and put into practice, *history* begins, and, although it is in the making, nowadays it is no longer merely a history of persons, institutions, or small groups producing various kinds of knowledge. It is a history in which we are all immersed in the evolution of modern industrial civilization and its transition to socialism, in which the intelligentsia—and with it all the various forms of knowledge, in particular science and scientific technology—will have a greater or a lesser role to play depending on the level of critical consciousness and the militance shown by the intellectual in the choices he makes, and on the resoluteness with which he goes about creating those cultural forces demanded by the historical situation in which we are living. The intelligentsia can refrain from being an isolated alien body within capitalist society or it may actually transform itself into a human factor of history in the making. Whether it will do one or the other is a question that would take us beyond the present discussion. The roads are open and the intellectual has a choice which he will have to make, whether he wants to or not, as the transition to socialism moves onward and as the historical channels for the reproduction of capitalist society and its model of industrial civilization gradually close.

Within the context of this complex historical situation, the importance of the critical and militant intellectual derives from his radical drive. By dint of circumstances, the intellectual becomes rootless, whatever his social origins or institutional ties, and thus ceases to define his relationship to society in terms of social status, prestige, or power within the system. He does not first place his intellectual roles and functions on the market, to decide thereafter the direction into which he can or must steer creative imagination, inventive thought, and the constructive utilization of man's cultural forces. In a word, the capitalist system of production and power ceases to count on him to realize its possibilities or meet its needs. The possibilities of making the move to socialism and of building a socialist society now enter into the picture and dominate his theoretical and practical thinking. On the other hand, this same radical drive forces the critical and militant intellectual to come out of his own skin, so to speak, and transcend the narrow human limits of the world of letters to seek true alliances beyond and above the relatively narrow concessions and bargains, some conscious, some less so, that are so destructive to the development of culture. It is prudent here to remember that if there did not exist divergent social groupings and contradictions among the dominant classes, as well as a class antagonism irreducible to any conservative formula *within capitalist society*, mankind would be doomed. Industrial civilization would be condemned to either stagnation or extinction. The critical and militant intellectual, in turn, would have no other alternative on the historical scene: his choice would have to be between surrender and suicide. Because the intelligentsia can choose, because history is the progressive "unfolding of the realm of freedom," the intellectual is able to opt for a mobilization of cultural forces that enter into conflict with conservative pressures, with the perpetuation of the existing order, and with the continuation of the capitalist version of industrial civilization. In doing so he is opposing and destroying his "use by the existing order," but by the same token he also becomes a dynamic link between present and future, a factor in the quest for a way out of the historical impasse weighing down on capitalism at both the center and the periphery.

The firm acceptance of a utopia, with all its intellectual, moral, and political implications, does not prevent the recognition of one point at least. In a country like ours, where conservative control of power is at once so entrenched and so violent, and where the bourgeois revolution had to throttle the cultural and political tempos of national revolution to achieve its own consummation, the space available for practice of utopia is very confined and the road of transition is proving to be rocky indeed. What intellectual radicalism found to be impossible does not promise to be easier for radical intellectualism. The conditions are worse and the intolerance even more extreme and more destructive. Moreover, in being "less instrumental" and "more dangerous," radical intellectualism will also be more visible to "the forces of the preservation of order." It must expect systematic persecution and relentless repression. These are the facts. We must recognize them, not to recoil, but to delimit our field of action and, within it, that which the critical and militant intellectual must do in the immediate future in Brazil.

Two basic tasks may be distinguished: (1) the intellectual will have to come out of himself, not just to seek allies but also to mobilize the surrounding cultural forces, which are to varying degrees politically polarized and identified with the broad democratic element within the national revolution; (2) for the moment his crusade should be openly and intensely directed against toughening of the existing order, i.e., against the form capitalist reaction has assumed in Brazil, namely, a protracted counter-revolution that is consolidating a brutal class tyranny, supported by an autocratic bourgeois state that is increasingly freer to expand its fascist components. How we shall accomplish these tasks is something we shall have to discover for ourselves. The most violent oppressive and repressive techniques invariably engender countervailing techniques that can neutralize and overcome them; at the same time they engender the most profound and critical movements of "revolution within the system" and "revolution against the system."

In this respect they do not "destroy historical options" but rather show the way to them. The present disorientation is the product of experience: the technology of oppression and repression already existed, having been part of the legacy of our slavocratic past and the long period of Republican *truce*. It was merely expanded and improved upon by the "transfer of modern technology" to the police and the military. The other technology (or counter-technology) is still to be learned or invented. Even so, the critical and militant intellectual must not neglect those tasks: he must remain alert to possible openings of democratic bourgeois radicalism, to contradictions of class interests under dependent capitalism, and to the eruption of pressures from below, from the working and destitute classes, since the fissures existing in dependent and underdeveloped capitalist societies make these tasks, which are so difficult at the political level, much easier at the cultural level. By establishing a new, open, profound, and constant relationship with these pressures from below, the intellectual will be able to throw himself with all his being onto the historical scene, not as a petit bourgeois stereotype of the "engaged intellectual" but as a connecting link between the protest of the masses and the genuinely democratic rhythms of the national revolution. On the other hand, he should also find here new grounds for participation in the socialist movement. Between 1940 and 1960, a parallelism was encouraged between the intellectual and political roles of the intelligentsia, but this has now become obsolete. The perturbations of history simplified the practical problem, since they abolished the reasons, apparent or real, for such a split in political attitude inherent in the self-assertion of the intellectual before society. Nonetheless, these things are happening *before* a more solid and mature socialist movement has emerged in Brazil. This means that though the path may not be easy, it must be opened by the critical and militant intellectual and that the responsible intelligentsia must direct its creative imagination in various directions simultaneously. What had been but a roadsign along the way is now the only exit. Either the critical and militant intellectual commits himself to strengthening and spreading the socialist movement, or he will remain a puppet in the hands of the cultural forces of preservation of the existing order.

Translated by Michel Vale

NOTE

1. Discussion of the ideological choices of conflicting bourgeois interests goes beyond the present exposition. The "liberal" and "conservative" polarizations are not so clear-cut as many thinkers would like to believe. It would also not be correct to claim that the oligarchy was unitary and was shut in upon itself, or that industrialism had no ambiguous characteristics. The liberalism of all the bourgeois sectors was irremediably conservative; and the conservativism of the agrarian interests, which gravitated in the direction of trade and the banks, possessed strong liberal components. Moreover, imperialist domination penetrated all polarizations and promoted a kind of conservative unification of liberal consciousness, which has always been instrumental for the external control of the economy and the proclaimed national revolution. The least that can be done is to avoid analytic simplifications, while awaiting a serious sociological study of the topic.

BIBLIOGRAPHY
SELECTED WRITINGS OF FLORESTAN FERNANDES

BOOKS

1949 *Organização social dos Tupinambá.* São Paulo: Instituto Progresso Editorial. 2d ed. rev. and exp., São Paulo, 1963.

1952 *A função social da guerra na sociedade Tupinambá.* São Paulo: Museu Paulista, 1952. 2d ed., São Paulo, 1970.

1954 *Apontamentos sôbre os problemas de indução na sociologia.* São Paulo: Universidade de São Paulo (Coleção Cursos e Conferencias, No. 3).

1955 (With Roger Bastide), editors. *Relações raciais entre negros e brancos em São Paulo.* São Paulo: Anhembi. 2d ed. rev. and exp., São Paulo, 1959. 3d ed., São Paulo, 1971 (title changed to *Brancos e negros em São Paulo; ensaio sobre aspectos da formação, manifestações atuais e efeitos do preconceito de côr na sociedade paulistana*).

1958 *A etnologia e a sociologia no Brasil; ensaios sôbre aspectos, da formação e do desenvolvimento das ciências sociais na sociedade brasileira.* São Paulo: Anhembi.

1958 *O padrão do trabalho científico dos sociólogos brasileiros.* Rio de Janeiro: Universidade de Minas Gerais.

1959 *A ciência aplicada e a educação como fatores de mudança cultural provocada.* São Paulo: Departamento de Educação, Serviço de Medidas e Pesquisas Educacionais.

1959 *Fundamentos empíricos da explicação sociológica.* São Paulo: Companhia Editôra Nacional. 2d ed. São Paulo, 1959. 3d ed. Rio de Janeiro, 1978.

1960   *Ensaios de sociologia geral e aplicada.* São Paulo: Pioneira. 2d ed., São Paulo, 1971.

1960   *Mudanças sociais no Brasil.* São Paulo: DIFEL. 2d ed. rev., São Paulo, 1974. 3d ed. rev. and exp., São Paulo, 1974.

1961   *Folklore e mudança social na cidade de São Paulo.* São Paulo: Anhembi.

1963   *A sociologia numa era de revolução social.* São Paulo: Companhia Editôra Nacional. 2d ed. rev. and exp., Rio de Janeiro, 1976.

1964   *A integração do negro na sociedade de classes.* Rio de Janeiro: INEP. 2d ed., 2 vols., São Paulo, 1965. 3d ed., 2 vols., São Paulo, 1978.

1966   *Educação e sociedade no Brasil.* São Paulo: Dominus-EDUSP.

1968   *Sociedade de classes e subdesenvolvimento.* Rio de Janeiro: Zahar. 2d ed., Rio de Janeiro, 1972. 3d ed., Rio de Janeiro, 1975.

1970   *Elementos de sociologia teórica.* São Paulo: Companhia Editôra Nacional. 2d ed., rev., São Paulo, 1974.

1972   *O negro no mundo dos brancos.* São Paulo: DIFEL.

1972   Editor. *Comunidade e sociedade no Brasil: leituras básicas de introdução ao estudo macro-sociológico do Brasil.* Sao Paulo: Companhia Editora Nacional.

1972   Editor. *Comunidade e sociedade: leituras sôbre problemas conceituais, metodológicos e de aplicação.* São Paulo: Companhia Editôra Nacional. 2d ed., São Paulo, 1973.

1973   *O capitalismo dependente e classes sociais na América Latina.* Rio de Janeiro: Zahar. 2d ed., Rio de Janeiro, 1975.

1975   *Universidade brasileira: reforma ou revolução?* São Paulo: Alfa-Omega.

1975   *A revolução burguesa no Brasil.* Rio de Janeiro: Zahar. 2d ed., Rio de Janeiro, 1976.

1975   *Investigação etnológica no Brasil e outros ensaios.* Petropolis, RJ: Vozes.

1976   *Circuito fechado: quatro ensaios sobre o "poder institucional."* São Paulo: HUCITEC.

1977   *A sociologia no Brasil: contribuição para o estudo de sua formação e desenvolvimento.* Petropolis, RJ: Vozes.

1978   *Folklore em questão.* São Paulo: HUCITEC.

1978   *A condição do sociólogo.* São Paulo: HUCITEC.

1979   *Apontamentos sobre a "teoria do autoritarismo."* São Paulo: HUCITEC.

1979   *Da guerilha ao socialismo: a Revolução cubana.* São Paulo: T A Queiroz.

WORKS IN ENGLISH TRANSLATION

1959   "Current Theoretical Trends of Ethnological Research in Brazil," *Revista do Museu Paulista*, 9, New Series.

1963   "Pattern and Rate of Development in Latin America," in U.N., UNESCO, Expert Working Group on Social Aspects of Economic Development in Latin America, *Social Aspects of Economic Development in Latin America.* Paris: UNESCO.

1967   "The Social Sciences in Latin America," in Diegues, Manuel, and Wood, Bryce, *Social Sciences in Latin America.* New York: Columbia University Press.

1967   "The Weight of the Past," *Daedalus*, 96 (Spring 1967).

1968   "Economic Growth and Political Instability in Brazil," in Sayers, Raymond, ed., *Portugal and Brazil in Transition.* Minneapolis: University of Minnesota Press.

1969   *The Negro in Brazilian Society.* Trans. by Jacqueline D. Skiles, A. Brunel and Arthur Rothwell. Ed. by Phyllis B. Eveleth. New York: Columbia University Press.

1970   *The Latin American Residence Lectures.* Toronto: University of Toronto.

1970   "Immigration and Race Relations in São Paulo," in Morner, Magnus, ed., *Race and Class in Latin America.* New York: Columbia University Press.

1974   "Beyond Poverty: The Negro and the Mulatto in Brazil," in Toplin, Robert Brent, ed., *Slavery and Race Relations in Latin America.* Westport, CT: Greenwood Press.

1977   "Slaveholding Society in Brazil," in Rubin, Vera and Tuden, Arthur, eds., *Comparative Perspectives on Slavery in New World Plantation Societies.* New York: New York Academy of Sciences.

1979   "The Negro in Brazilian Society: Twenty-Five Years Later," in Margolis, Maxine, and Carter, William E., eds., *Brazil: Anthropological Perspectives.* New York: Columbia University Press.

1979   "Foreword," in Evans, Peter, *Dependent Development: The Alliance of Multinational, State and Local Capital in Brazil.* Princeton, NJ: Princeton University Press.

ABOUT THE AUTHOR AND EDITOR

Florestan Fernandes, since 1977 a full professor of sociology at the Catholic Pontifical University of São Paulo, was educated in the Faculty of Philosophy, Sciences, and Letters of the University of São Paulo, where he taught from 1945 until his forced retirement in 1969. He has also held appointments at Columbia University, the University of Toronto, and Yale University. Fernandes is the author of more than twenty-five books on subjects ranging from folk culture and race relations to economic development and class organization.

Warren Dean received his PhD from the University of Florida in 1964 and is now a full professor of history at New York University, specializing in the economic and social history of Latin America. Previously affiliated with the University of Texas-Austin, he has also taught at Princeton University, Columbia University, and the University of São Paulo. His many publications include *The Industrialization of São Paulo* (1969) and *Rio Claro: A Brazilian Plantation System* (1976).